Corvette Odyssey

CORVETTE ODYSSEY

**The True Story
of One Man's Path
to Roadster Redemption**

TERRY BERKSON

THE LYONS PRESS
Guilford, Connecticut
An imprint of The Globe Pequot Press

As a boy I used to go spear fishing at night in a creek that ran near the edge of town. A mantle lantern provided light but due to the water's deflection the fish were never where you saw them—you had to make an adjustment to hit the mark. The same principle has been applied to this story. Also, some of the names have been changed for obvious reasons.

The Lyons Press is an imprint of The Globe Pequot Press.

Printed in the United States of America

ISBN 1-59228-294-6

Text design by Casey Shain

1 3 5 7 9 10 8 6 4 2

The Library of Congress Cataloging-in-Publication Data is available on file.

Contents

For Alice, Elizabeth, and Jonathan

In memory of police officer Joe McCormack

who was killed in the line of duty.

"All you can ever ask from the worst of experiences is

that they deepen our knowledge of the tragic."

—Norman Mailer (in a letter to me back in 1982)

Corvette Odyssey

the DREAM

I KEEP HAVING THE SAME DREAM. I write it
down here in my journal. It's not exactly a dream because I
haven't quite dozed off when it starts. I'm not sleeping much
because the baby wakes up to be nursed every couple of hours.
The kid's crying makes me feel like a chain is being dragged
through my insides. I haven't told my wife about the dream
because I haven't told her that the car's been stolen. Why make
her feel bad when she's just given birth?

The dream goes something like this. The car's out in the
street—all banged up. It lies there like a wounded animal. It's
been ripped open and is being disemboweled by three bald-
headed men. They have thin mustaches and are wearing
sneakers. One rips things out and two are carrying them away.
The one tearing out straightens up to rest. There's grease on
his bald head and the back of his neck. His legs are spindly
under black pegged pants. I want to go there to twist his head
around but I don't know where this is happening. My dad is
standing close by but he doesn't say or do anything.

The dream fades away and I start going over the details of
the theft: where I parked, who was around, which way they

might have gone, who might have seen something. This time I think of a hot dog vendor at the curb nearby when I parked. I'll have to ask him if he remembers the car. You can't miss a red, '63 Corvette convertible. There's not a time I drive it that someone doesn't stop and ask me about it or admire its condition, which I'm proud to be responsible for. This rehashing of the theft and variations of it go on in my mind every night before I get to sleep.

It was still early when I walked across the backyard. A light breeze passed through the long branches of the willow tree. Bert started barking because he thought he was going for a run in the park but I told him no and his ears dropped in disappointment. I pushed the weathered garage doors open, their bottoms dragging across the cement like snowplows, the glass windows vibrating. New doors, I added to my mental list of things that had to be done around the house. I'd been out of work for several months so there was time to fix things but no money. Jimmy Carter had said the economy was getting stronger but that didn't seem to help the magazine business. I slid behind the wheel of the station wagon and glanced over at the Corvette when my eyes got used to the darkness inside the garage. It was covered with a layer of dust that gave an orange hue to the normally bright red paint. Lately I was feeling pressured to sell the car. The money it could bring would pay the hospital bills for the baby as well as for some needed repairs on the house and for a new heating boiler in the cellar. Several people had urged me to get rid of the old roadster, but I couldn't bring myself to put an ad in the newspaper. I got out of the wagon, walked around, and pushed open the other two garage doors so that I could back the Vette out. There was plenty of time; I'd be able to wash it before I drove to the hospital.

I pulled out the hose and got a bucket of hot water and mixed in some Ivory Snow from the kitchen. First, I wet down the car with a gentle spray of cold water. Then, I threw the hot, sudsy towel from the bucket onto the roof and began to scrub in a circular motion. I did the washing in sections, rinsing off the mild soap right away so that it wouldn't leave any streaks. To make a car look really clean, you have to wash places that can't be seen, like under the bumpers and in the grooves of the rocker moldings. It's the reflection from the hidden areas that makes what you see even shinier. When the car was clean I dried it with a chamois by dragging the leather across the top and hood and fenders. Finished, I put the hose and bucket away and backed out of the driveway.

Tony the house painter waved from his bench on the porch across the street. He was retired and could take it easy now that his three daughters were all married off.

The Corvette always seemed to run better clean. The spinners cast the reflection of the sun on the houses and buildings we passed. A kid elbowed his friend and pointed to my car. I thought of having to sell it and dismissed the idea by thinking of my beautiful new baby boy.

There was a parking spot about a block from Victory Memorial Hospital. It was just down the street from the entrance to Fort Hamilton at the end of Seventh Avenue in

Brooklyn. There were lots of people around. I engaged the reverse choke, the cut-off switch, and the alarm as I had done for the past twelve years and headed for the main entrance.

Alice's half sister, Benita, was in the room holding the baby. She was thirty-one, a few years older than my wife. She took care of her for a time when they were younger. I knew she didn't want me to marry Alice. She kept putting up these flaming hoop obstacles. Now, she was always filling Alice's head with advice and steaming her up about "all those fishing trips" I took. She didn't understand that if you freelance for an outdoor magazine you have to know what you're writing about—so you go fishing. Anyway, most of the time I took my family with me. She was one of the people pushing for the sale of my Corvette.

Benita showed me the baby as if I had nothing to do with his being there. "You don't have a cold or anything?" she asked, drawing back.

"No," I said, annoyed.

"Give him the baby, Benita," Alice commanded. "He's the father." It felt good to hear my wife go up against her sister.

I put my index finger in the baby's hand while thinking about hospital bills. He gripped it tightly as if to say, I'm gonna be around for awhile. I thought, soon he'll be baiting his own hook. I pictured us standing in a stream fly-fishing together. My boy.

"Don't we make nice kids?" Alice said to her sister.

My wife looked radiant and proud with her blue eyes glowing and her long, bay hair let down the way I like it. It fell across her eye and she puffed at it from the corner of her mouth. She cooed at the baby and nudged his cheek with her high-bridged nose. After awhile a nurse took him back to a glass-enclosed area. I reported the last-minute touches I had made on the new baby's room. Our three-year-old Lizzie was staying at my cousin Charlie's house while I did the painting. I'd been laid off from work as an electrician since the beginning of the summer. Before that I was writing for a fish and game magazine but it didn't pay enough so I fell back on the trade that had helped put me through school. Then things got tight, even in construction.

When visiting hours were over Benita said she was going to take a cab back to Manhattan.

"Terry'll give you a lift to the train," my wife said as a matter of fact. "It'll save money."

We kissed good-bye and I checked out the baby in the nursery once more before leaving with Benita. It was a beautiful September afternoon. We began to walk down the block. Benita's long neck, short black hair, and sharp features made her head look like it was hovering when she turned to speak to me. She was nice looking but not in the same way as Alice. My sister-in-law was now a fashion designer. We rarely talked because our conversation usually wound up like a debate. To avoid trouble, I kept up a light exchange. "Is your boyfriend still taking flying lessons?"

"He also likes fast cars," she said.

The Corvette didn't seem to be where I parked it. I'd had this feeling a thousand times before. We walked faster, Benita with her long legs trying to keep up with me without showing effort. I started to run, leaving her behind. Then I stopped and turned back. "Maybe we passed it."

"Maybe," Benita said lifting her shoulders. She walked back toward the hospital with me. She was beginning to get impatient while I was getting frantic.

"Maybe I'm mistaken about where I parked." I stepped into the street and looked in both directions.

Benita looked at her watch as two guys in a tow truck passed by. They were laughing and seemed to look at the spot where I had left my car. I wanted to run after them but they were moving fast. I made a mental note of their license plate number.

At a phone booth I dialed 911. The number rang about ten times before someone picked up.

"I want to report a car stolen."

"Hold on," a woman said. When she finally got back to me she wanted to know everything, including whether or not I had an innie or an outie for a belly button.

"Can't you send a squad car instead of wasting all this time?"

"Sir, I have to get this information."

While I was on the phone, Benita kept looking away impatiently. "I have an appointment," she kept saying. Finally, she got a cab. I was glad she was gone. I wouldn't have to act calm. I kept walking from the phone booth to the parking spot, hoping that somehow my car would appear. I called my cousin Charlie at his shop and asked him to come down. He said he was in the middle of a job.

The police arrived two hours later. "Where the hell were you?" I asked. They looked annoyed at the question. Maybe if they had responded right away they could have radioed an alarm. An old Corvette would have been easy to spot.

The cop in the passenger seat had a pad. He took down the information printing very slowly.

"Aren't you going to put an alarm out for my car?"

"We don't do that right away," the other cop said from behind the wheel.

"Oh, you wait till it's too late."

"We have to make sure the car was stolen."

"That's crazy! Of course it was stolen—how come you took so long to get here?"

"Cool it, pal, or you'll have more problems than just a stolen car! You know how many cars are taken in Brooklyn every day?" he said. "Two or three a week from this hospital alone."

"But, this isn't a regular car. This isn't just transportation! This is a collector's car! I've had it for over twelve years!"

"Well, the insurance'll take care of it."

"I'm not insured. How about putting out that alarm?"

"Take it easy," the cop said. He didn't seem to understand or care. I didn't expect him to but had to tell him anyway.

My cousin Charlie arrived before the police left. "I had to finish the job," he said. I thanked him for coming and got into his car. We cruised around the neighborhood on the chance the Corvette had been joyridden and then dumped. I told him about the guys in the tow truck but I had already forgotten one of the numbers on the plate.

"It was probably your imagination," Charlie said.

"I don't think so."

He turned on the CB radio attached to the bottom of his dash and put out a call for my car. I had always thought CBs were unnecessary toys but now I was taking his radio seriously. It was hot driving so we stopped at a grocery to pick up a six-pack of beer.

We rode around Brooklyn for several hours, checking out all the known dumping grounds for stolen cars. The effort seemed feeble but it helped to relieve all this nervous energy that was building up. If only I had left the Vette home. Charlie invited me to his house for something to eat. He was the same age as me, but had no children yet. I had planned to go there to check on my daughter anyway. I noticed how patiently he was driving around. Well, he should be, I thought. He's gone enough miles in that car. Wish I had a nickel for every race we've been in together. These days, better make it a quarter. Nickels aren't worth anything anymore. I couldn't believe my Corvette was gone.

REWARD

IT WAS ALREADY DARK when Charlie and I quit driving around, so he took me home where I could get my station wagon to follow him to his house. We took our shoes off before entering. His wife, Florence, was a real fanatic when it came to cleanliness. "You're just in time to put your daughter to sleep," she said. Later, Lizzie complained that my bedtime story was too short. "When's Mommy coming home?" she asked for the tenth time.

I was finding it hard to concentrate. "Tomorrow."

"With a new baby?" she said, her big brown eyes wide.

"Yes, a new baby. So, go to sleep. Tomorrow's coming soon."

"Okay, Daddy."

I didn't tell her about the car for fear she'd tell Alice. At the table I ate without tasting until Charlie remarked on how big Jack was. "Eight pounds ten ounces!" he said. "You could've won a pool." He was trying to make me feel better as he did when we were kids and lived in the same house and I often stayed upstairs with his family because my mother was forever in a hospital and my dad worked long hours in his taxi.

"You did have the car for twelve years," Charlie said. "You can't say you didn't get your money's worth."

"It's not only the money."

"Nobody gets a car like that back."

I knew this was true because I'd heard plenty of stories about stolen Corvettes and how you never see them again.

On the way home after leaving Charlie's, I was thinking about what kind of rat would steal a car from outside a hospital. A hospital! The gall made me so angry I pounded my fist into the dashboard. Then my fingers started to throb and I was worried that I had broken something. I remembered one dumping spot that Charlie and I had overlooked. It was down by the Coney Island Creek off Cropsey Avenue. Pieces of stolen Corvettes always used to be scattered in the high weeds near the water. Over the years I found a gas tank, a rear spring, a bumper, and more. In ten minutes I was in Coney Island.

My Plymouth bounced over the dirt road that led down to the creek, the headlights showing the way. There was a late-model Camaro still in good condition except it had no wheels. What a waste to ruin a whole vehicle just to steal the tires. In a couple of days the vultures will have it stripped clean. I pulled up to another car hidden in the weeds. The plates and tires were still on it. There was a strong odor of gasoline as heads bobbed around in the weeds behind the car. They were about to torch this one. I threw the Plymouth into reverse and backed away seconds before the Camaro exploded into flames.

Then I saw the guys jump into a waiting car and they took off. It must have been an insurance job.

I knew an American Indian who hung around the creek when we were kids and I had a rowboat down there. He still lived nearby. Not long ago Charlie told me the Indian was in his store to have a key made, that he was retrieving cars for finance companies. "Theodore tracks them down and steals them away from people who aren't making their payments," Charlie said. It paid good and it was legal. Maybe the Indian could tell me how to find my car.

In the morning, I went to the Sixty-eighth precinct before picking up Alice and the baby from the hospital. My fingers were still sore from pounding on the dashboard. Losing your temper worked against you. "Any news about my car?" I asked.

"What car?" the sergeant behind the high desk said.

"The Corvette that was stolen near Victory Memorial Hospital."

"There's a lot of Vettes stolen. You got a case number, buddy?"

"No. They didn't give me one."

"They were supposed to. Now, I have to drop everything to look it up." He came back with the case number. It was 8880. "You don't have to come in any more," he said. "We'll call you."

"These two guys in a tow truck looked suspicious. I got their license plate, all but one number."

"We can't do anything with an incomplete number," he said. He was having coffee with a jelly doughnut and the powdered sugar was on his chin. What did a lousy car mean to this guy? It wasn't something alive. I pictured a stranger behind my wheel. "You wanna take some advice from me?" the sergeant said with the jelly floating around in his mouth. "Forget about the car. Cars like that don't show up again— not in one piece they don't."

I gave the cop a nod and headed for Victory Memorial.

At the hospital we took pictures before leaving for home. Together we held the baby as the nurse clicked away. I was putting on this shit-eating grin and wondering if it was transparent, wondering if Alice suspected anything. We had been getting along. She might have thought that something was wrong between us. I was about to tell her when the nurse handed the camera back to me. My wife was glowing. I couldn't tell her—for at least a couple of days.

After I settled Alice and the baby into the house I phoned the Indian. He said, "I don't know how you've held on to the car this long."

"You got any ideas on how I can track it down?"

"It's probably been cut up. They get $2,500 just for a nose," he said.

"I can't believe they'd destroy such a clean car."

"They do it to new Cadillacs." He didn't offer much hope but he gave me a couple of ideas. One was to check around the neighborhood gas stations and car hangouts close to where the Vette was stolen. I pictured him at the other end of the line, the receiver dwarfed in his big hand, his wide face calm. "Let them know that there's, say, a $500 reward out for the car. And try reward posters and an ad in a newspaper."

It felt good to talk to the Indian. He gave me some traction. Theodore was always the idea man when we used to hang around the creek. "Keep me posted," he said.

"Who was on the phone?" Alice asked.

"This guy wants an estimate for some rewiring."

The next day I printed up a reward poster and had a hundred photocopies made. It read like this:

REWARD

$500 for information resulting in
recovery of 1963 Corvette convertible.

Red with black rag top. Car in original
condition. Must be close to same.

Lost on Mon. Sept. 17 Bet. 2:30 and 3:30 P.M.
at 7 Ave. near 92 St. (Victory Memorial Hosp.)

Lic # 107YXO Mod # 30867S114730

No Questions Asked

Tel: 256-9366

I tacked the posters to trees and poles all around the area where the Vette was stolen, and, handed one to the hot dog vendor, who didn't remember anything. They let me put a couple on the bulletin board in nearby Nathan's drive-in, and several gas stations in the neighborhood posted the reward in their windows. I also hit some police stations and all the auto supply stores I could think of, even on the other side of Brooklyn. Putting up the posters drew a lot of curious observers. Many of them had had their own cars stolen, but no one knew anything. Most people were pessimistic about my getting the car back. One guy in a junk shop on McDonald Avenue told me how they cut through a case-hardened lock like butter to steal his son's racing car. He had also put up a reward but the car was never seen again. I felt pressured to do as much as possible before getting called back to work. Then I wouldn't have time to do anything.

"Where were you for so long?" Alice asked when I got back.

"I was making that estimate."

"Think you'll get the job?"

"I don't know."

"We could sure use the money."

The phone was ringing. I was tired of not being able to sleep. Tired of the rerun playing in my mind, tired of seeing the empty parking spot and waiting forever for the cops to come. I jumped out of bed so the ringing wouldn't wake Alice and the kids but the baby was crying even before I got to the phone. Alice was alarmed by the middle-of-the-night call.

"We got your car," a guy said sloppily. "Come down and get it."

"What is it, Terry?" Alice called from bed.

"Wait," I told her and then asked into the phone, "What kind of shape's it in?"

"Good shape," the guy said. "We towed it in from the parkway. Just come down to TACO Collision on Dahill Road."

"Did you call the police?" I asked. But the phone clicked dead in my ear.

"Who was that?" Alice wanted to know. Then I told her everything. She took it better than I had expected. In fact, she talked about how much money the car was worth. I thought of a long, slow, rainy trip we took through the Adirondack Mountains, puddles slapping hard against the floorboards, the wipers pushing the water away, the steady drone of the engine.

Dahill Road was close by so I wanted to check out the body shop right away.

"But it's the middle of the night!" my wife said.

"I can't wait till morning."

"Be careful. They could mug you for the reward."

"They'd be crazy to think I'd carry $500 around with me."

"They won't know if you have it or not."

"Don't worry. I'll be right back."

In ten minutes I was on Dahill Road. I stopped in front of the place and cut the engine. TACO looked closed. I got out and peered into the window anyway. There wasn't even a light on. A Ford Galaxy with dark tinted windows stopped in the intersection nearby. There were no other cars around. I sensed the driver was watching me. It was very quiet and I could hear his engine idling. It would have been nice to head him off and find out who he was. After a minute the car raced away. Maybe they wanted to get a look at me, to know who was coming after the Corvette.

KING KONG'S CAVE

WHILE HEADING EAST on the elevated part of the Belt Parkway I used to see this large tract of land bordered by the Narrows and the Brooklyn Army Terminal. There would always be abandoned cars hidden in the tall grass. The cars were easy to spot from up on the parkway. I figured this was a good place to check out but when I tried to get to it there were high fences, buildings, walls, and roadways blocking my entrance. I circled around to Fourth Avenue and Sixty-fifth Street where the N train surfaced from the tunnel. I had Bert with me. He was an Irish setter and all wound up and ready to go for a good run but there were No Trespassing signs all over the place. A police car was parked and working the corner for red-light runners. I walked over to the cops to ask how I could get into the field. Bert jumped up on the door as the cop at curbside rolled down his window. I yanked the dog down with the leash but not before the red-headed officer gave me a dirty look.

"How do I get in there?" I asked pointing.

"For what?"

I told the cop about my Corvette. He seemed interested and explained how I could gain entrance. "They dump a lot of cars down there," he said. "The kids call it King Kong's Cave."

"Why's that?"

"You'll see," he said. "Have you tried NATB?"

"No. What is it?"

"National Auto Theft Bureau," the police officer said. "They might be able to help you."

"Thanks for the info," I said, heading for my car. I drove down to the train tracks the way the cop told me, Bert barking all the while, and followed the rail bed until we couldn't go anymore without doing damage to the car. Then I let the dog out and locked the doors as Bert bucked like a bronco to get loose. We walked along the tracks and drifted over to where the N train comes out of the ground. We entered a tremendous superstructure with huge columns. It looked like it was about two or three blocks to the other side, which was marked by the bright light of day. My eyes had to adjust to the darkness created by this labyrinth of big cement-covered beams and walls and struts. I spotted the first stolen car tucked away in a corner. It had been completely stripped—a Riviera. Then, there was another and another, all late models. Car parts were scattered like the bones of prey the giant Kong had brought back to his lair. What a great place for crooks to work, I thought. All they need is a light and tools and they could dismantle anything without being disturbed. The columns seemed to support the

street and the land over the subway as well as the Gowanus
Expressway before it ran into the Belt Parkway. I reined Bert
in like he was some ferocious beast when I spotted three
grease-smudged guys approaching. One of them was completely bald, as in my dream.

"You see any old Vettes down here?" I asked as Bert
pulled toward them.

"We ain't seen nothing down here," the bald guy answered
without breaking stride. They were probably taking a lunch
break from whatever they were up to. I looked over my shoulder after a few seconds to find them looking back at me. Maybe
they were worried I'd find and steal their dismantling tools.

Like the cop had told me, the other side of the cave
opened onto the field I had spotted from the elevated road. It
was about three in the afternoon, a warm late September day.
The smell of the weeds and the summer-dried grass reminded
me of the country. I let Bert loose when we were a couple hundred yards from the cave. In no time he was on the trail of a
rabbit that darted across my path. You could follow Bert's direction by the movement in the tall grass.

After checking out several cars, I came upon a burned
Corvette just off the path. It was easy to spot because the whole
car is made of fiberglass, which leaves a white residue when it
burns. It was completely stripped. All that was left was the
chassis, which looked like it could be from a '63 Corvette. A
sadness settled in me. After stalling for a few minutes I
scratched the rust off the ID on the frame. The numbers
weren't mine.

I heard splashing in the weeds about fifty yards off and went over to find Bert swimming in the flooded foundation of what must have once been a house. The stench from the swamplike water was terrible. Bert climbed out and walked up to me shaking the stinking water from his coat. "Get away!" I told him. His tail went between his legs but he had an innocent expression on his face. We walked back through the cave and then along the tracks but I had to wait until he dried in the sun before we headed home or else he would have stunk up the car.

"What's that smell?" Alice asked when I entered the kitchen.

"I took Bert for a run and he . . ."

"There are a lot more important things you could be doing right now."

"I know."

Every day I left in the station wagon, unsure of where I was headed. Sometimes I just cruised around aimlessly and let myself get lost in unfamiliar neighborhoods waiting for a sense of direction or something.

I placed the ad for the reward in two weekly newspapers, the *Selling Post* and the *Home Reporter.* When they hit the stands I got a lot more phone calls. The *Selling Post* attracted informed characters, but the *Home Reporter* brought calls from people who weren't sure what a '63 Corvette looked like.

I kept thinking about a book my father once read to me. I heard Dad's voice calm and almost expressionless: "Then the boy tracked the pony's hoofprints in the mud." The little horse had been sick and somehow it got out of the barn and was caught in the rain. And when the boy found his pony and fought with the bloody vultures, my seven-year-old mind thought that the pony would stand up again, but he didn't. He was lost. Irretrievably lost.

In what my dad later referred to as his "impetuous forties," we left Brooklyn one summer and headed for Richfield Springs to stay with my father's older brother, William, and his wife, Ruta. For a time Charlie had visited too, but mostly it was just me and Dad. One afternoon, Dad returned to Uncle William's, his car steaming after a long trip. "I bought a farm," he announced as we all sat at a big round oak dinner table.

"A farm?" Uncle William said. He looked shocked. "You don't know the first thing about running a farm."

"I'll learn," Dad said.

I remember going to see the place and sitting on the running board of the Buick having strawberries and cream as Dad talked with Miss Bowmaker, the owner. She had picked the berries herself. They were sweet and cool and I rubbed their rough skins on the roof of my mouth. I could tell they liked each other, Dad and Miss Bowmaker, the way their eyes would catch. She was a schoolteacher and was selling the farm because her father had died. She spoke softly and had long light-brown hair with streaks of gray in it. She wore thick plastic glasses that matched her fair skin, and when she'd close her mouth after talking, it was as though one soft lip was caressing the other.

Later, Dad played some songs for her on the upright she had in the parlor. The room felt warm and cozy with two stained-glass lamps burning. I stood next to the keyboard holding on to the side wood. The backs of Dad's hands were veiny with high knuckles and the fingers were long and rectangular. I didn't know all the names and all the words then, but the music pulled at my insides and made me want to pound on the keys alongside him. I didn't though—cause Miss Bowmaker was there. He started with "Doll Dance." I always liked the intro to that one, the way the rhythm builds. Then he played "Kitten on the Keys" and then "The Kiss Waltz" and then another and another, and he played "Pick You Up in a Taxi, Honey," as I called it then, his foot hitting the pedal at a steady beat, the heel of his shoe pounding at the floor, making the lamps shake, his sure hands dancing across the keyboard almost faster than I could see.

He ended the tune sweating. Miss Bowmaker was sunk into a stuffed high-backed chair with her long legs crossed and a faint smile on her face. During the next song an ash from the Lucky on Dad's lip fell between the keys. She got up to brush it away and their hands mingled for a few beats. He finished the session with "The Rosary." I knew that was one of his favorites because he'd sing it at home sometimes:

> The hours I spent with thee, dear heart
>
> Are as a string of pearls to me . . .

the BIRD LADY

THE PHONE CALLS KEPT COMING. One guy rang up and said he saw a '63 Corvette on the news. It was shown in a police auto theft bust. The guy sounded straight. I checked it out with the police auto squad but they said no '63 Vettes were recovered, only newer cars.

"Anyway," the cop added, "We come up with your car, we'll call you."

I had my doubts about this. If the numbers were removed from the car, they couldn't trace it to me. My Corvette could sit in the pound for a few months and then go up for auction to some lucky insider.

When I heard the news on the radio about the same bust, the police said they recovered one hundred fifty cars, but in talking with them on the phone it slipped out that the number of cars actually recovered was much less. They made a big splash in the newspapers from time to time to placate all the people whose cars have been stolen. The police couldn't control all the stealing. It was open season for car thieves.

I get a call from a lady. She was very sympathetic. "I'm sorry to tell you this, but a car like the one you describe in the newspaper was on my block for several days."

"A Corvette?"

"Yes. The kids broke all the windows and some guys were taking parts off it and then finally the car was burned."

She sounded sincere so I wanted to go over and show her some photographs. Alice had taken them in the spring when Lizzie was helping me wash the car.

The lady's apartment was on Eighty-fourth Street near Fifteenth Avenue. There was a parking spot across the street from her building. I checked myself in the shiny brass mailbox before ringing the bell and saw a two-week growth of winter beard. I was wearing my work dungaree pants and jacket and a ragged ten-year-old camouflage hat. I ripped the hat off and stuffed it into my pocket before pressing the button. She answered the door in her bathrobe without looking alarmed.

"Excuse the way I'm dressed," she said. "I just got out of the shower."

I entered and stood in the hall. She was pulling both ends of her bathrobe together, a nice-looking woman in her early forties, blonde and slender with high cheekbones and a little bit too much makeup for just coming out of the shower.

"I know how you feel," she said looking into my eyes. "That car was very dear to you."

I whipped out the photographs and showed her one. She brushed against my arm, her nipples sticking out like jujubes through the thin bathrobe. "That looks just like the car," she said. My heart dropped. "Is that your little girl?"

"Yes."

"You're blessed."

I showed her all the pictures. She was positive it was the car and described its destruction. "At first it was beautiful," she said, "only it didn't have wheels."

"How did it look after they burned it?" I asked. "I mean, did all the paint come off?"

"I know how it feels to lose something dear to you," the woman said. She was looking into my eyes. Her robe slipped open revealing that she was not really a blonde. "I had a parrot that died a couple of months ago," she said. "I'm still getting over it."

"But, how did the car look after it was burned?"

"Would you like a cup of coffee?"

"How did it look?"

"You know, I had my parrot cremated. Would you like to see the ashes?" She put her hand lightly on my butt.

"Not really. What about the car?"

"Yes. All the paint was burned off and the fenders were scorched."

Now, I knew she was mistaken or lying because if the Vette had been on fire the fiberglass would have burned right down to the chassis. She saw in my eyes that I no longer believed her and the expression on her face turned to anger or maybe determination. Her teeth were clenched and her lower jaw was protruding as I sidestepped toward the door. She was annoyed that I hadn't picked up on her advances. Her robe fell open from six to twelve o'clock. I turned and reached for the doorknob expecting it to come off in my hand. She grabbed on to the tail of my jacket and said, "Where're you going?"

"I just remembered I'm double-parked."

She stopped me from opening the door all the way. "Come back if you need to talk."

"I'll keep it in mind." We played tug of war for a few seconds, her hands covering mine on the knob, until I managed to slip through the opening and out into the hall.

It was wonderful to be with Dad every day while waiting to buy the farm. At home, six days a week, he was out driving the taxi, and on Sundays he would go to the hospital to visit my mother. Sometimes he would bring her home for a dreaded visit and invariably there would be a violent fight with a lot of screaming and she would break all the dishes and the windows and tip over the furniture. Often I worried from behind a closed door that she would hurt my father. Now, Dad took me swimming and rowing on the lake. One afternoon we walked out into the pasture and lay down in the cool green grass. We wrestled. His one good eye was smiling. I tried to hold his arm down but his hard-boiled egg of muscle triumphed. Dad didn't cough as much in the morning as when we were in the city.

There was a rushing brook, a wide rich green lawn, and wild flowers all around the house with a hand pump well out back. The trees were very tall, almost frightening, and formed an archway to the entrance of a faded green barn. The next thing I knew, Dad moved us on to a boarding farm near Good Year Lake not far from Miss Bowmaker's. "We'll stay here until we move to our farm," he told me.

You do a lot of dumb things when you try something new. I never tried to be a detective before. The effort feels closer to writing than to electrical work. I picture Mickey Spillane tracking down a car. Maybe doing this in itself was dumb, but I was learning little by little. After a while I could tell over the phone if I was wasting my time talking to someone. People like to bullshit you. Maybe they get a laugh out of it, maybe it makes them feel smart or important. Anyway, I just heard them out and dismissed the nuts and the phonies. Some of them were pretty convincing. I went on more than one wild-goose chase. When nothing happened I upped the reward to $1,000. It was a lot of money but I had to do it. Anyway, where can you get a '63 Corvette for $1,000?

Actually, the roadster didn't cost much more than that twelve years before when I first bought it. I had been having all kinds of problems with my '55 Ford and was spending more time under it than in it. After paying tuition, there wasn't enough money left to pay a mechanic to do the necessary work. My father gave me the green light to look for something reliable—a Volkswagon, two or three years old. While searching, I tripped over the Vette and fell in love immediately. There was a little body damage to the nose and front fender but mechanically, with minor exceptions, the car was in good condition. I told my father about it. Maybe he was back in his impetuous forties mood because he said, "Sounds like a good car for the price."

The next day, I went to the police station and had the vehicle identification numbers checked to make sure the car was not stolen. It came up clean. Then we went to the bank and my father took out twelve hundred of his hard-earned dollars. I was to pay him back when I could.

When I drove the Corvette home, I wasn't sure how owning a car like this would affect my studies. Maybe it would be too much of a distraction. There it was, low and shiny under the leafless willow tree. I felt like I had made some kind of commitment that would last a long time—a through-thick-and-thin type of thing. I was stunned in kind of the same way I was years later when I got married—happy and a bit frightened. The Vette's power, compared to my '55 Ford, was awesome. I'd turn the key and the car would come alive—all three hundred horses. Sometimes I'd put my ear to the hood and listen to the engine cooking, the metallic sound of the timing chain, the whir of the pulleys, the breath of the fan, the lifters clicking away. Dad and I took a ride to the Pennsylvania Dutch country. He was impressed with the Corvette's speed and maneuverability. He held on to the grab bar, his knuckles getting white, as we tooled around a sharp curve on the narrow blacktop. We stopped at a roadside stand to buy homemade bread and cheese from a bonneted Amish girl and had a little picnic on the side of the road. Horses were grazing in a field of timothy nearby. "Let's stay on a farm for a couple of days," I suggested.

"No. I'm worried about the house," Dad said. He had lived there almost his whole life.

"We're locked up good," I assured him.

"You didn't have to round corners."

"What?"

"We used to walk straight through the fields to the new subway. Ours was the only house on the block. Did I ever tell you that?"

"A hundred times, Dad."

"Different neighborhood now. Locks on the doors. Never had 'em for forty years. People like one big family. They used to drag me out of the house to play at Pellegrino's Bar around the corner, and feed me beers until it felt like I was playing with boxing gloves on. Did I ever tell you that?"

"Yeah, Dad. The house'll be okay."

"Let's just go home."

"We drove all the way here just to turn around and go home?"

"We've seen it."

I don't know why my father didn't want to stay in the country. Maybe it had to do with getting older and being less flexible and feeling more at ease in a familiar chair. I was disappointed that he wouldn't take advantage of the good country air that would have let him breathe better.

There was an unexpected problem with the insurance. Fire and theft in Brooklyn would cost $300 a year—not including liability. In 1968 this was a lot of money, 25 percent of what we paid for the car. I knew I couldn't afford this and would have to do without it. Anyway, money couldn't replace the Corvette. Instead of the insurance, I installed several antitheft devices that, three times over the years, prevented the car from being stolen. One time I pulled a crack addict out of the car. He had slipped behind the wheel while it was running for inspection in a service station. He just ran away.

I was always careful where I parked and never left the Vette on the street too long. At home, Bert was on guard ready to devour any trespassers.

The house was constantly filled with friends and neighbors wanting to see the new baby. They meant well but it was exhausting to have people around when you wanted to let it all hang out. Some, like Tony the painter, were helpful or at least let me feel easy, but then there was snoopy Mrs. Filo who was just interested in what the inside of our old Victorian looked like, and gabby Josephine whom I had to help up and down our weathered front steps. I offered her a cigar when she was leaving but she refused. Benita came every day. She straightened up the place and cooked some meals that literally got stuck in my throat. She had a way of aggravating me. She complained about the old-fashioned stove and sink we had. "Your refrigerator's too small," she said, and "why don't you buy your wife a dishwasher?" If she didn't succeed in aggravating me, the kids did with their crying, which always seemed to start at meal time. I was out in the backyard trying to relax so the food would go down when I heard the phone ring inside the house.

I saw Benita through the kitchen window. She picked up the receiver, talked briefly, and then hung up.

"Who called?" I asked when back inside.

"Oh, somebody about your Corvette," Benita said while shoveling food into my daughter's mouth.

"What'd they say?"

"He didn't say anything. I told him he was calling in the middle of dinner and that he should call later."

"Why didn't you get his number? I could've called him back."

"What am I, your secretary? I do enough around here."

"Who asked you?"

"Cool it, Terry," Alice said. "Benita's been a big help."

"Please, don't answer the phone anymore."

"Suit yourself," Benita said.

I spent the next day like the day before, cruising around Brooklyn, hoping I'd spot my car. Alice tried to tie me down with chores and things to fix and shopping lists I'd never fill correctly.

I finally located the tow truck that I saw that first afternoon when the Vette was stolen. It was just by chance while I was driving down to the hospital to see if I could catch any more cars being clipped. It belonged to the Friction Towing Company. I watched the gas station where it parked for a couple of days but never saw any suspicious cars being towed in. While trying to trace the license plate of the tow truck, I spoke on the phone with a Mr. Tamerack from the National Auto Theft Bureau that the cop at King Kong's Cave told me about. He was helpful and gave me a couple of ideas on how to hunt down a stolen car, but he couldn't really assist me because his organization was supposed to work with insurance companies only.

"I don't think you have much of a chance," Tamerack said before hanging up.

a FLAG in BUSHWICK

ABOUT A MONTH AFTER my car was stolen, I got a call from a school bus driver named Nick. He said he saw a '63 Vette several times while on his route. "The reason why I remembered it," he said, "is because a car like that don't belong in a bombed-out neighborhood."

"Are you sure it was a '63?"

"I ought to know, I got one myself. The guys down at Nathan's showed me your reward poster. I wasn't even gonna call. You know. What's the odds on it being the same car? But it didn't fit into the neighborhood. It stuck out like a flag."

He sounded like he was telling the truth. It might not have been my Corvette he saw but this was something to check out.

"Was the car automatic?" I asked

"I couldn't look inside."

I had to see this guy face-to-face. We arranged to meet at Nathan's on Eighty-sixth Street in a half hour.

"One last thing," he said to me. "You got a pencil?"

"Yeah."

"I got the license plate number. It's 938PVX."

"Wait, the point broke!"

"Take it easy, pal."

I was on my way out the door when the phone rang again. It was Benita. "Hello, Berkson," she said. "Get called back to work yet?"

"No, I didn't get called back to work yet."

"What are you doing?" she asked.

"Nothing, why don't you come over?"

"What's the catch?"

"No catch. I'm going out. You can visit with Alice."

"Where're you headed now?"

"I got a date."

"I wouldn't be surprised."

"Yeah."

"Tell her I'm coming."

"My date?"

"No, dummy, Alice."

"Okay. Here, tell her yourself." I handed the phone to Alice and gave her a squeeze good-bye.

When I got to Nathan's, it was about to rain. Nick was waiting in this big Riviera. Even behind the wheel I could see that he was some kind of body builder. He had his girlfriend in the car. She was eating a hot dog and didn't say a word.

"Where's your Corvette?" I asked.

"I don't drive it when it looks like rain."

He seemed wary, like he was talking to a kook or maybe he thought I was a cop. It took him a few minutes to loosen up. I learned that he'd seen the car three or four times outside this garage near the corner of Stagg and Lorimer Streets.

"I never heard of either street."

"They're not too far from the Williamsburg Bridge," Nick said. "Toward Bushwick."

"If it's the car, you got the reward."

"I'm not interested in a reward. I got $25,000 wrapped up in my car. I'd kill anyone who'd try to steal it. I feel for you."

"Do you think it would be there now?"

"I don't know. I only pass there during the day on my bus route."

"I'd like to check it out."

"Now?"

"Yeah, now."

He shook his head to his girlfriend and started telling me how to get to Stagg and Lorimer, but then we agreed to drive there and take a look. It was about a twenty-minute ride in my car with Nick sitting up front and his girlfriend in the backseat with a bag of french fries. Nobody said much on the way.

When we got there, Nick showed me just where the Corvette was parked the three or four times he saw it. There was a garage across the street with a big "A" on the door. "One time," Nick said, "I saw a guy get out of the car and walk to the garage."

I was dying to look inside but it was closed. It started to rain. I planned to come back the next day, alone.

"When I stopped the bus to take the license number some guys were watching me," Nick said on the way back to Nathan's.

"I hope that didn't scare them off the street."

That night, I have the dream again. They're ripping things out and carrying them away. I still don't know where this is happening. I'm left wide awake so I sit up to read for awhile. The light rouses Alice. "Did the baby wake you?" she asks.

"No."

She moves close to me. "When am I getting laid?"

"Isn't it too soon?" I say.

"Yes."

"I thought so."

"You fool. I'll rub your back. That always puts you to sleep."

In a short time I feel like an alligator having his belly rubbed. I see the Corvette up on four jacks and me underneath on a creeper. Alice is waiting in the driver's seat for me to tell her what to do. "Pump 'em," I yell and she responds by pressing on the brake a half dozen times. "Now hold it!"

"Okay," Alice says, "but if the meat loaf burns you're going to eat it."

I open the bleeder on the wheel cylinder and a bubbly spitting stream of brake fluid shoots out. "How's it feel now?" I ask.

"Higher, but still spongy."

"Pump 'em up again and hold!"

"Terry, couldn't we do this after dinner?"

"It'll be dark."

◆

In the morning I called Mr. Tamerack and asked him if he could run the license plate number that Nick had given me to see who the car was registered to. I had given up on the police helping me out because they had just about told me to get lost.

"I'm really not allowed to do this," Tamerack said.

"But the cops won't help me either."

"I can't . . ."

"Just press a couple of buttons for me."

"Well, we're kind of old friends by now," he said pensively. "I'll make an exception just one time."

The car came up registered to a Luis Rubio, 25 Ten Eyck Street, Apartment 3G, Brooklyn, New York. I pictured it parked right in front of the guy's house and me slipping my key into the unchanged lock.

"Now, this doesn't mean it's your car," Tamerack said. Then he interpreted the vehicle identification number. "It's a red '63 Corvette convertible."

"With automatic transmission?"

"Yes."

"It's got to be my car!"

"There were lots of cars built like that," he said.

I knew this was true but many of them were wrecked or stolen and cut up. I rarely saw a '63 Vette on the street. Most of the survivors were in the hands of collectors or were strictly sunny Sunday cars. Judging from the condition of the neighborhood where Nick spotted the Vette I doubted if Rubio was a collector.

"I'm sticking my neck out by giving you this info," Tamerack said. "I wouldn't want you to do anything foolish."

"I'm not a hothead."

"People lose control."

"Not me."

"If you see the car call the police."

"Right."

STAKEOUT
on "A"

IT WAS ALREADY OCTOBER. We were in the midst of an Indian summer. I was on the Brooklyn-Queens Expressway taking the same route that Nick had taken the night before. It was still morning. The sun was out and I knew it was going to be a hot day. Twenty-five Ten Eyck Street turned out to be only two blocks from the garage with the big "A" on the door. There were only a couple of buildings on the street where number 25 was standing. The rest must have been leveled by demolition crews, leaving large open lots blanketed with bricks and debris. Here and there were clusters of green where weeds and ailanthus trees had shot out of the rubble. A good part of several blocks in this area has been knocked down leaving a large open plot with buildings sparsely placed.

When I didn't see my car in a few passes around the block and several adjacent streets, I parked the wagon and entered number 25 Ten Eyck to look for Rubio's apartment but there were no names or numbers on the mailboxes. Knocking on doors and naming names would definitely alert Rubio so I left the building trying to think of another angle to locate him.

Back in my car, I drifted past the big "A" on Stagg Street. There were several men at the corner nearby. Two of them were sitting on milk boxes. There was also a motorcycle, a tow truck, and a van parked just across the narrow street from "A." I took the plate numbers of the tow truck and the van without being conspicuous like Nick was. The men hanging around took no particular notice of me as I stopped at the corner.

Just then someone came through a man-sized door in "A" and hopped into the van. I saw this through my rearview mirror. He was skinny, with a mustache, and had a white hand-kerchief tied around his head. I wanted to take a look inside the garage but couldn't think of an excuse that wouldn't be obviously snoopy. I parked around the corner and sat on the brick fence of a building where I could see anything that went down Stagg Street, which is a one-way street. I waited the rest of the morning and except for a run to a grocery to get something to eat, a good part of the afternoon.

Nick's bus came down the street. He was craning his thick neck until he spotted me before making the turn onto Stagg. He stopped and opened the front door as I walked toward him. I had some Vette photos that I forgot to bring to Nathan's the night before. Nick and his helper looked at them as I stood on the steps of the bus. There was a faint odor of urine. I looked back at the kids and saw that they were all retarded. One girl stood up in the aisle and Nick yelled, "Hillary, you idiot, get back in your freakin' seat!" His helper, who was about eighteen and had greasy spiked hair, walked back and pushed Hillary into her place.

"As far as I can see, it's the same car," Nick said. "But, I don't remember it havin' front bumperettes like in these pictures."

"Yeah," his helper agreed.

"They could've taken them off," I said. "The plate number you gave me checks out. It's registered to a car exactly like mine, right down to having an automatic transmission."

Of course the car could have been altered since it was new and no longer match what its numbers described, but I didn't want to think about that.

Nick continued on his route. I hung around for the rest of the afternoon and even walked down Stagg Street past the garage with its big old patched and paint-flaking green garage doors and the man-sized white "A" that might have been part of the address or the name of something. The motorcycle was parked outside and several men were standing on the corner. They seemed to look casually in all directions for a hot car to enter or leave. I figured they were neighborhood idlers who were glad to help out the "A" operation. The door to the garage was closed so I didn't see a thing. At least one police car cruised through about every fifteen minutes. If I could just get a look inside.

I came back the next day and saw nothing except two freshly painted cars that stopped at "A" for a short time. The driver of one, a Charger, pulled a roller jack out of the garage and raised his car to tighten an exhaust pipe. I thought of later knocking on the door and asking if I could borrow the jack to fix a flat tire, but if the guys hanging out on the corner were some kind of lookouts, they might have spotted me because I had passed several times by car and on foot and my jack excuse could sound lame.

I made two trips down to Bushwick over the weekend. The weather was beautiful. It must have been hot as hell in that garage but it remained closed. If I could just pass by at a time when they opened the big door to "A." I was sure I'd see my car sitting there. This made me pass down Stagg Street many times. Even if they knew I was watching, I might catch them with the door open. I also checked number 25 Ten Eyck Street but only the tow truck was parked there.

The station wagon I was driving was a Plymouth. It had the squeakiest brakes you ever heard. They announced my arrival on Stagg Street every time. The metallic shriek made the fillings in my teeth feel loose. Everybody in the neighborhood must have noticed me. I had the impression that they all knew each other. Cars seemed to have been driven a couple of blocks and then parked again. Many houses remained standing on some streets in this mostly demolished neighborhood. There was the sound of radios everywhere and a lot of car washing going on. All this activity mixed my senses as though I had a fever. Rupert Holmes and Hank Williams Jr. were on my radio singing about piña coladas and family tradition. I switched to a Spanish station to fit in better. There were a few late-model Corvettes in the area. They always seemed to be parked outside one of several makeshift garages scattered around the neighborhood. I doubted that any of them would clear a going-over by the auto squad.

There was a baseball bat under my seat. It was a comfort to know it was there. If I saw the Vette on the street I was going to sit on it, no matter what, until a police car passed.

When I was a kid my father kept this big old black Buick up on blocks in the backyard for several years. He had driven it for a time but it had a big engine and used too much gas to be a taxi. There was a spare tire set into the front fender and a partition separating forward and back compartments. You could slide the glass open horizontally if you wanted to talk to the driver. There were two round folding seats next to the partition wall. The seats and all the upholstery were made of a maroon-dyed leather. The car had actually been a limousine but Dad used it as a cab for a while and the hand-wound trip meter was still mounted up front. My gang and I logged many miles in that car. The guys would pile in the back as I'd flip down the flag on the meter. The initial charge then was a quarter. We made a trip to Canarsie on a rainy day when there was nothing else to do. The rain beat on the roof as the meter ticked away. Bugsy and Roger were behind me rubbing the fog off the back window.

"Step on it!" Bugsy yelled, his eyes bulging. "The cops are coming!"

"Yeah!" the others echoed. I whipped the wheel around and yanked on the shift stick. We all made screeching noises as the rain drummed on the huge engine hood and the wide whitewall tires stood motionless just a half a foot off the ground. Then Roger got locked out—no—thrown out, and the rest of us were inside laughing as he pressed against the window like a drowned rat, his glasses tilted on his nose, begging for shelter.

Once a year Dad would let the Buick down and get it started, not without a lot of trouble. It was always a group effort. Charlie's father and a couple of other guys on the block would help push it out onto the driveway. They'd inflate the tires and trickle gas into the carburetor. There was always some expense during the revival and one time Pie Face Freddie at the gas station told my father, "Get rid of that load. It's a sinking ship!"

I felt bad for Dad and the car.

"Just do a temporary repair on the gas tank," my father told Freddie, "so I can take it for a run."

Then the car was finally rolling and I was on the front seat next to Dad as he went through the gears. Seeing him happy like this made me feel older like I knew something that he didn't. He looked over at me with his hands gripping the wheel tightly as the car surged ahead.

"Feel the power! Can you?"

"Yeah, Daddy! Let's go faster!"

The annual start-ups lasted for several years, each time my father vowing to restore and maintain the big powerful car. Then he skipped a year and when he finally tried to start it there were too many things wrong and one rainy day late in winter a tow truck dragged the old Buick and all my future trips to Canarsie out of the yard but not before the bumper caught the thick hedges on the drive as though the car knew it was going to the glue factory. I stood watching from a rain-splattered window and thought of being angry with my father after the junk man paid him and he came inside the house all wet and muddy, but he was too sad to see the car go and instead we sipped hot tea together and ate pieces of hard rye bread smeared with orange marmalade.

Years later I found the Buick's trip meter hidden in a corner of the cellar and dug it out and wound it up and put the flag down to hear the old familiar ticking, and for a moment the rainy days and the start-ups and the make-believe trips were all with me.

On Monday, to get away from the squeaking brakes, I took my bike out of the garage and secured it to the roof rack on the Plymouth with a piece of rope. Alice came out of the house with Lizzie just as I finished tying it down.

"I want you to do some shopping for me," she said.

"Now?"

"Unless you want to eat eggs again for supper."

"I'll stop on my way home."

"I need Enfamil right away, for the baby."

"I thought you were nursing."

"My breasts are sore and I'm not letting down enough milk."

"How long has this been going on?"

"All along. That's why the baby cries so much."

"Okay, I'll just run down the corner to the grocery."

"Joe's a lot more expensive."

"I know, but I have to leave."

"Where're you going?"

"Just for a bike ride."

"Take me for a bike ride, Daddy!"

"Not today."

"When, Daddy?"

"Soon."

"When is soon?"

"Maybe tomorrow."

I got the shopping delay out of the way and headed for Bushwick. Hidden under my seat were a couple of hats and shirts to change off so it didn't look like the same guy was passing down Stagg or Lorimer all the time. Alice was better off not knowing what I was up to.

I parked a few blocks from "A" and lifted the bike off the roof. There was so much glass in the street that you had to weave down the block as in a slalom. I peddled past the garage at a moderate speed not to attract attention. The door was closed as usual. After several circuits I returned to the car and changed my olive drab T-shirt and camouflage hat for a faded maroon shirt and a blue denim cap with a red band. I tried a new bike-riding posture, which was leaning well over the handlebars as opposed to riding in an erect position. For the next change I'll go up and down with my head as I petal—I see a lot of guys ride that way. Damn it! I just wanted to barge through that door in "A," spot my car, and call the police, but there were a lot of guys connected to "A": the lookouts on the corner, the owners of the vehicles always parked outside, the drivers of the newly painted cars—the whole neighborhood seemed to be involved. I had the feeling that if I went inside "A" I might not get out, except maybe in a trash bag. I was fairly sure that they knew I was around. One time I passed I heard what sounded like a chain saw going in the garage. I'd heard stories of Corvettes being cut up with chain saws. I was almost to the end of the street when a gray Chevy slid around the corner, engine screaming, tires smoking. It was headed straight for me, so I jumped the curb and crashed into some garbage cans as it raced past. I picked up my bike and just stood there for a while, my heart pounding. Maybe the driver was a nut or maybe they were trying to scare me off.

Later in the afternoon, I couldn't stand waiting any more. There was a police car stopped at a gas station three blocks from "A." I approached the cop at the wheel and began to tell him about how a car like mine was seen on Stagg Street and traced to 25 Ten Eyck but I couldn't get to see it. McCutchin was on his nameplate. He believed my story.

"You mean "A," he said.

"You know about it?"

"We got orders to leave that place alone."

"Why?"

"Eh," he said shrugging his shoulders. "They want to get the big fish. The auto squad must be on it—but that's off the record."

"Sure." I told him about Luis Rubio and how I didn't find the name on the mailboxes. He offered to check it out for me while I waited in the gas station but after twenty minutes he returned with his quiet partner.

"The numbers on the doors are all mixed up," he said. "We couldn't even find apartment 3G. We checked with the superintendent. He don't speak English. He says he never heard of Luis Rubio."

"Maybe it's a phony name."

"My shift's over in an hour," McCutchin said. "Meet me at the precinct house. It's only a few blocks from here."

I wasn't sure if telling the police about Rubio did any good. I wouldn't have asked the superintendent about him like they did because that would definitely tip him off.

I got a better look at McCutchin at the station house. He was about forty years old, had a receding hairline, sharp features framing small fast eyes, and stood about five ten. He took the information I had gotten from Tamerack at NATB and with some objections from the cop in charge of the computer, ran the 938PVX plate number that Nick had given me. There was a lot of noise in the building. It was wall-to-wall cops.

Predictably, the '63 Corvette description came up along with the name Luis Rubio and I thought we were back where we started.

"Look at this," McCutchin said pointing to the screen. "This car was registered less than a month after your car was stolen."

Then he asked the computer for a printout on all Luis Rubios with driver's licenses in New York State. This seemed like a good idea but a few minutes later the machine spit out scores of Luis Rubios. I had visions of checking all over the state. McCutchin scanned the names and matched a birth date, 8/24/51, with the Rubio connected to the 25 Ten Eyck Street address.

"It's gotta be the same guy," McCutchin said.

Considering the attitude of most of the cops I had met so far, this cop was the best thing that ever put blues on. The Luis Rubio with the same birth date was listed as living in Stony Point, New York.

"Maybe that's where they're keeping my car."

"The code on the printout shows that he got his license by mail. That might mean that he's living in the city and using an upstate address, or it might mean nothing."

McCutchin also ran the plate number of the tow truck that was parked outside "A." It came up registered to a Roberto Perone who lived about fifteen minutes fron Stagg Street. The Corvette could also be there. I intended to check this address out too.

"Be careful," McCutchin said, "and let me know how you make out."

That night Charlie called and asked if I wanted to go fishing in the morning. I told him about some of the progress I'd made in searching for the Vette. He was surprised that I was still looking. "Maybe you're getting a little too wound up over the loss of a car."

"I just have to check out some leads."

"They're really biting out by the Ambrose Tower."

"Nah, I gotta go to Stony Point tomorrow."

"You're wasting time. You're laid off. You could be painting the house—or fixing the bricks on the front stoop. Someone's gonna fall, you can be sued!"

"Yeah, I know."

ENGORGED

IT WAS THE FIRST OF NOVEMBER and my boss was overdue at calling me back to work. I was glad the recession had slowed construction and the need for electricians. I might have tried working for the magazine again but the idea of sitting at a desk made me squirm.

"There were two more phone calls today," Alice said at dinner. The kids were in the living room and not crying for a change. She relayed what the callers had to say.

"They don't sound worth following up," I told her.

"Good, then maybe we can talk about something else—like hospital bills."

"I don't mean to put you through this."

"But you do," she said with anger in her voice.

"Oh, come on," I said reaching across the table and pressing her hand. Her eyes filled with tears. I got up and took her in my arms and she winced when I squeezed. "What's the matter?"

"My breasts are sore." She opened her blouse to show me. They were all red and chapped and irritated. "They're engorged," she said.

"How'd that happen?"

"I don't know. Benita says stress can do it. The baby's merciless trying to get enough milk out of me."

"Then, why don't you stop nursing?"

"Mother's milk is better than formula," Alice said with tears in her eyes. "I feel they're full but it hardly comes out—even with a breast pump. It's painful."

"I had no idea," I said holding her as she began to sob. We stayed like that for a long time. "You want me to call the doctor?"

"He'll tell me to stop nursing."

"Why torture yourself? Maybe I can relieve the pressure."

"What can you do?" Alice said.

"I could try."

"Okay."

We sat at the table and I placed the horn on her breast and gently squeezed the rubber bulb on the pump. We were able to extract a bit of milk from one breast but the suction was irritating and only making things worse. Then I got a large salad bowl out of the closet and tried coaxing the milk out with my fingers. This was more successful and before long a tiny pool of milk was beginning to form at the bottom of the bowl. When my fingers grew too forceful and caused pain, Alice complained, "Hey, you're not bleeding your brakes here!"

We both laughed at the sound of the milk shooting into the bowl. I stopped for a moment and kissed her tenderly. That seemed to make the milk come out better. The puddle was even getting a little foamy. But in the end we really didn't get that much milk out. The next morning we called the doctor and he told Alice to bind her breasts to stop milk production.

Two days later, after signing for my unemployment check at Dean Street, I drove up to Stony Point. It was about thirty miles north of the city. I expected to see my car sitting in Rubio's driveway. Instead, I found four high priced cars parked in front of a new house in a nice suburban-type development. One car was a brand new Corvette with the name Rubio on the license plate. It was still early morning and there was a light rain falling noiselessly on my windshield. There was a garage under the house. My roadster was inside for sure. When I saw it I'd call the state troopers, but to avoid the slow response I got when the car was first stolen, I drove to the trooper headquarters to make them ready for my call.

The young, lanky officer I told my story to seemed impressed that I'd traced the car this far.

"All I want from you is a quick response so they can't move it before you get there."

"We're not New York City," the officer said in answer to my complaints about how slow the cops were in Brooklyn.

On the way back to Rubio's place I saw his brand new Corvette coming from the opposite direction. I drove on to his house. There were no windows in the garage or I would have gotten out and taken a look inside. I parked the wagon across the street and waited. About fifteen minutes later Rubio's

Vette returned. He got out with a bag of groceries and a newspaper under his arm. He was about five eleven with a large drooping mustache, a big face with a long fat nose, and bushy brown hair. He had spindly legs, a slim hipline, and was in his mid- to late twenties. I looked at the police computer printout that McCutchin had given me. This guy fit the Rubio description to a T, so now I knew exactly what the enemy looked like. He turned and faced me when he reached the top of the steps to his front door. I looked right at him. I would have loved to get my hands on his throat. He seemed to wonder what I was doing there and then disappeared inside the house.

I hung around for a while and then left to get something to eat. The weather broke by late morning and it turned out to be a nice day. Later, I passed by Rubio's place but there was no change in the position of the four cars. I cruised down Main Street and before making my turn, spotted a red '63 Corvette pulling into the parking lot in front of the bank. I made a quick U-turn and raced down to where the car had parked but kept my distance. There were no hubcaps on it and no bumperettes but it looked like my car. I grabbed a phone nearby to call the troopers. It seemed to take forever to make the connection but once I got through they were there in three minutes. I approached the Corvette with the tall, friendly officer I had spoken to earlier. The closer we got the less it looked like my car. When next to it, for sure it was not my car. I was embarrassed. "Sorry," I said to the state trooper.

"No harm done," he said, but I knew I had blown my credibility with this guy.

"I still think I'm on the right track," I told the officer.

"We'll check it out—if we spot a '63 in Rubio's driveway."

I knew if I approached Rubio about the car it would be destroyed, so I just had to be patient. I passed by his house once more but there was no change. Then, I headed back to Brooklyn disgusted with myself, tired of playing detective, wishing I had the money for another Corvette—just to help forget about mine.

I made only a couple of trips down to Stagg Street during the next two weeks. I was sure that when Nick took the license plate number they saw him and now they had the car stashed somewhere, or else they already cut it up. But I still couldn't believe they'd destroy such a beautiful car.

I called Nick to find out if he had seen anything new. His old lady told me that he wasn't home so I left a message for him to call but he never got back to me. I figured he was tired of the whole thing. He wouldn't have been if it were his car.

One windy night when I finally got to sleep, some cats started yowling in the alley where Bert couldn't get at them. I turned on the lamp and went over all the information I'd gathered. Still, I couldn't be absolutely positive that the car registered to Rubio was mine. After a while I turned out the light and just lay there thinking.

◆

There were two brothers on the farm where Dad and I were staying. The older, who was my age, was called Weenie. He was skinny and blond and he had a big brown birthmark on the side of his face just below his temple. Dad took me and Weenie and his little brother to see this pony he wanted to buy. He didn't say he wanted to buy it but somehow I knew and I told my friend.

"You don't even have a place to keep 'im," Weenie said.

"You'll see," I told him.

It was a little black pony and the guy who owned him wasn't around. Dad walked out into the paddock and took the pony by his mane and led him over where we were waiting next to the barn. Inside, big horses were whinnying and kicking at their stalls. I was worried about the angry horses kicking their way out and that the owner might be mad that we were riding without permission. Dad gave us each a turn as he walked the pony around. When it was Weenie's turn the little horse went into a fast trot and got away from Dad. Weenie was bouncing up and down and swaying from side to side as the pony chopped along.

"Help, help!" Weenie yelled.

"Whoa," my father kept calling.

It was funny to watch Dad taking these long strides to catch up with them. He caught on to the pony's mane and was dragged along for a time before he was able to slow him down. When they returned, Dad's quiet thin face was pale and he was breathing hard.

Some time not long after that we went back to Brooklyn. Dad kept the farm for several years without us ever living there. When he'd talk of selling it I'd beg him not to. Maybe he had fooled himself into thinking Miss Bowmaker would be around. Maybe to him, the farm wasn't the same without her. Maybe he just wasn't cut out for the country. Then, one day it was gone and I never saw it or the pony again.

"If you were older and could've helped me run it, I would've kept the farm," my father once told me. He was never handy like me with tools or equipment. I always pictured him more comfortable behind the wheel of his taxi or seated at the piano on a hot summer night with the windows open wide, the curtains dancing in the breeze, a Lucky Strike stuck to his lower lip.

I'll be down to get you in a taxi, honey
Better be ready 'bout half past eight!

In the morning I called Mr. Tamerack from NATB to let him know how things were going. After talking with him for a long time he put me in touch with Detective Pete Rousseau from the Police Auto Crime Unit. At first I thought I was getting the brush-off.

"Tamerack's a good friend of mine," Pete Rousseau said.

I told him about how the car was seen on Stagg Street, registered only three weeks after mine was stolen, and that it hadn't been sighted since the bus driver openly stopped to take the plate number.

"There's a good chance it's your car," Rousseau said. "But remember, there were a lot of cars like that back in '63."

"I know, but how many are left?"

"They already changed the vehicle ID numbers once. That's the best chance you got. They won't change them again."

"How come?"

"It's not easy to change a VIN. They'd need another tag and they're hard to come by. Just hang in there. As long as we have the numbers, the computer can locate the car anywhere in the country."

There were lots of interruptions in our conversation. The cop seemed swamped in auto theft business. "Just keep checking," he said.

"That ain't easy."

"What do you mean?"

"Do you know how hard it is to walk into a local precinct and ask to have a number run into the computer? Guaranteed, the cop at the front desk says no. Then, I have to explain the whole thing, and if he's totally convinced that I'm straight, he'll refer me to a detective who wants to hear the same story all over again and then maybe he might check the number!"

"What can I say, kid?"

"Isn't there a note or something you could give me to avoid the hassle?"

"Computer information's confidential. If it gets into the wrong hands—"

"But I'm no crook!"

"I know that but headquarters doesn't and rules are rules."

"In other words I'm on my own."

"When I think of it I'll check the number for you, but we're busy people down here."

"I know."

"Gotta go, kid. Call me if anything develops."

"Yeah."

INDIAN
TRACTION

THAT NIGHT, AFTER SUPPER I told Alice that I
was taking a drive down to the creek where the Indian lived.

"I wanted to visit my sister tonight," she said.

"Please, not tonight," I said. "I feel restless."

"So do I. I'm stuck home with the kids all day while you
cruise around. You're their father."

"I'm not enjoying myself."

"Neither am I."

"Why don't you go out tomorrow night?"

"Maybe my sister won't be available."

"Call her."

"All right, but I'm getting tired of being stuck home all
the time. While you play detective."

It was almost dark when I turned off Cropsey Avenue
onto a neglected, curbless pothole-infested street. The
Plymouth's suspension groaned as it bumped along slowly, the
brakes squeaking as usual. A Thunderbird was parked in the

lot next to the Indian's house so I expected him to be home. His family had lived here since the time when the Coney Island Creek ran all the way to Sheepshead Bay and Coney was really an island. My headlights showed that there were several cars parked in the backyard. I got out, climbed the wooden stairs to the porch, and tripped the knocker on the Indian's door. His loose-skinned mother answered without showing that she remembered me. She looked weak and much older than the last time I saw her. Theodore once told me that his mother could see things. Maybe she could see where my car is. She was breathing through her mouth. I decided not to ask her to use her powers.

"Hi, is Theodore home?"

"He's in the cellar. Walk around back," she said.

I found him at his bench working on a speedometer.

"Terry," he said calmly.

"Hello, Ted. I thought you were only repossessing cars."

"Used cars are a sideline."

"But the mileage?"

"I'm just fixing it," the Indian said getting back to his work. He'd changed since the last time I saw him. Looked older, gained a little weight, which made him look brawnier than ever. I wouldn't want to meet up with him in an alley trying to repossess my car. I told him how things were going. He wasn't impressed with the progress I'd made, but he gave me some ideas.

"Send a letter to this Rubio character," he said. "Write Address Correction Requested on the envelope. That could take you back to Ten Eyck Street, or Stony Point or another place the car might be."

"Sounds good."

"And check the insurance code number from the computer with AAIP."

"What's that?"

"Association of Automobile Insurance Plans. They can give you the insurance company what's his name—"

"—Rubio—"

"—Rubio uses, and tell whether he went through a broker or not. If he got his insurance through a broker there might be a forwarding address or something in the broker's office."

Another thing Theodore told me was to get into the police computer and find out if the new VIN had been unregistered for a long time. "That," he explained in his quiet way, "might show that this new identification for your car was taken from an old wreck or junker whose description your car happened to match. If this is the case, you're probably after the right Vette." His instructions were so methodical that when I turned to leave I felt a new confidence and energy.

"Bumped into Charlie," Theodore said. "He told me you don't fish anymore." As kids all three of us fished off Norton's Point near the mouth of the creek.

"Not lately. How about you?"

"I do some—could I interest you in a Camaro, real cheap with low mileage?"

"I'm holding out for a Corvette."

He laughed.

◆

Now, I had the Stony Point possibility covered by the state trooper, and Stagg and Ten Eyck Streets covered by Nick, McCutchin, and myself. These seemed the most likely places for the Corvette to be.

Nothing came of the address-correction-requested idea. I just got my letter back. A friend who worked for a newspaper put me in touch with a Detective Frank Daniels of the auto squad. This was a different outfit from the auto crime unit that Pete Rousseau belonged to. Daniels's office seemed to deal with car theft and recovery. Rousseau's with insurance fraud, but I had the impression their jobs overlapped. I knew I was bothering Rousseau calling so much. A lot of times they told me he was out when I knew he was there. One time he asked me if I got big phone bills. So, I started fresh with Daniels, not telling him about Rousseau, and vice versa.

Because of my newpaper friend, Daniels agreed to check out the history of the new VIN from the license plate that Nick the bus driver copied down. This information was on file in Albany. A week later he called.

"The VIN's been inactive for eight years," he said

"That's great!"

"It was last attached to a car owned by one Hector Malinda. I can't get a current address on this guy."

"So, it's my car I'm after."

"You can't be sure, but there's a good chance. I'd like to talk to Malinda. I'll get back to you if I locate him."

◆

66

On one of my routine checks with the computer and after the annoyed cop at the desk guaranteed that I wouldn't find out anything new from the same old VIN, I learned that the Corvette was now transferred to one José Fernandez on DeKalb Avenue in Brooklyn. There was already an alarm out for this guy's arrest. I went through the same routine of checking out the address that I did with Rubio and came up with nothing.

Now two guys had registered the car without altering the VIN. Pete Rousseau had been right. They weren't going through the trouble of changing the identification again. With no more leads the only thing I could do was wait. At the same time Alice was on maternity leave and wanted me to be out making money, but then how would I be able to look for the Corvette? My boss phoned the house but I hadn't returned his call because I was afraid he'd pull me back to work. The unemployment payments were running out. They didn't carry us but they helped. Paying the hospital bill almost wiped us out.

It was late afternoon. I was in the backyard working on the Plymouth, trying to get the squeak out of the brakes with a lubricant you put in back of the pads, when Bert jumped up from his sleeping spot next to the woodpile in response to the telephone ring in the kitchen. Alice was out with the kids so I made a dash for it.

"I've been trying to get you all day," this guy says. "I'm calling long distance from New Jersey."

"What can I do for you?"

"Did you put the reward in the *Selling Post* for a '63 Corvette?

"Yeah."

"I'm a used-car salesman. Some guy came in earlier today wanting to sell this Corvette that resembles the car in the paper. I told him that I wasn't authorized to buy cars on my own but that my boss would be back tonight and he could take a look at the car if it was brought in again."

"What'd the car look like?"

"It was a red '63 convertible, but without some details I can't be sure if it's yours."

"Was the guy Spanish?"

"Yes."

"Did you get the license plate number?"

"No, I didn't think of that."

I gave the man three easy things to look for: a quarter-inch crack on the extreme right of the windshield, a small cut in the third pleat in the back of the driver's seat, and a hand-stitched convertible back window. Most are laminated but I installed a new window with Alice's help. We used forty-pound-test fishing line for thread. It turned out really nice. I also gave him the new vehicle identification number that came from the car that Nick spotted on Stagg Street.

"That should do it," the salesman said to me. "If he comes in and it's the car, I'll get back to you."

"Wait a minute. What's your name? Where are you located?"

"Sam Ashkin, at Fort Lee Motors," he said, before hanging up.

Something seemed wrong. I checked Fort Lee with telephone information but there was no listing. The operator said she remembered a Fort Lee Motors but the company must have moved or gone out of business. What a fool I was. The guy had given me a phony business name. Maybe he already bought the car and was checking to see if it was the one with the reward out on it. The name Sam Ashkin started to sound like Sam Asking. Oh shit! It's the dumbest thing I've ever done. I should have been more cautious. If he has the car, he knows I have the new VIN. He'll cut it up or retag it for sure!

Naturally, Sam Ashkin didn't call back. The next day I headed over the George Washington Bridge, the windshield wipers not doing a very good job. Lately the weather was mostly overcast and rainy. Indian summer had long since passed. I pulled into a dealer at Fort Lee, my brakes still squeaking, and asked a guy in the office if anyone had been trying to sell him a '63 Corvette. The answer was negative so I left one of my reward posters with him to tack up for the other salesmen to see. I figured this Sam Ashkin character must be familiar with the area since he knew the name of a dealer that once existed. It might have been a coincidence that he picked a real name. He might have been calling from Brooklyn for all I knew, but there was a chance that he and the Vette were still in the area so I stayed with it, my eyes scanning back lots for a glimpse of the car's Riverside Red paint.

I stopped in more than a dozen car places in Fort Lee and adjacent towns. Each one took my reward poster and most were interested enough to say they'd keep an eye out for the car. The rain was light and steady all day. The feeling that I'd gone on another wild-goose chase set in. I pictured Rubio standing on the steps with his bushy mustache and spindly legs and wondered if the Vette might have been in his garage the day I watched his house in Stony Point.

Back in Brooklyn, when I entered the kitchen I heard Alice on the phone with Benita.

"Is your sister bugging you again?" I said for Benita to hear.

To my surprise Alice got off right away. She was very excited. Benita must have really got to her. "I don't know if I can take much more of this," Alice said. "I'm a nervous wreck. Why don't you call home sometimes?"

"What's wrong?"

"This Spanish guy called three times. He said the only one he wanted to talk to was you. He said he had the car, that he was supposed to be trying it out, but that he would deliver it for the one-thousand-dollar reward, no questions asked—and no police."

Lizzie came scuffing into the kitchen and crashed into me. "I'm hungry, Daddy," she said holding on to my leg.

"Wait, Liz, I'm talking to your mother."

"But I'm hungry now!" She opens her mouth wide. "Look, I'm empty."

"All right," I said heading for the fridge with her still wrapped around my leg. "I'll get you a carrot." When I scraped the skin into the sink instead of the garbage, Alice gave me an angry look. "That's right, clog up the drain."

Lizzie took the carrot and ran back to the television in the living room as I cleaned out the sink. "Go on!"

"I promised him I wouldn't call the police—all you wanted was to get the car back, I told him. But you weren't home and I didn't know where you were. I was sure you'd pay the reward if the car was yours. 'It's the car! It's the car!' he kept saying. Then he said, 'I don't have much time. I'll call you back.'

"I phoned your cousin Charlie. He couldn't believe that anyone would be crazy enough to deliver a stolen car for a re-ward, but he agreed to come to the house because I was so nervous. I thought I should go to the bank just in case the guy showed up with the car, but Charlie told me no, the guy would have to be crazy to come around and it could be dangerous for me to carry the money. 'You don't know who you're dealing with,' Charlie said."

Alice stopped talking for a minute as she lifted a pot of boiling potatoes off the stove and drained the steaming water into the sink. She puffed her hair away from her eyes. "You mash," she said putting down the pot and handing me the tool.

"So then what?"

"What about butter and milk and . . .?"

"Yeah, I'll put them in."

"Now!"

"Okay, go on!"

"The guy with the car called back once more before Charlie got to the house. He was disappointed that you were still not home and swore again that he had the car. 'I'm standing here in the phone booth looking at it,' he told me. I lied to him that I had the reward money. He told me, 'There better not be a double-cross.' Then he took down the directions to our house. He said that he was up in Harlem and that he would call when he was in our neighborhood. Who needs this aggravation? I was so nervous I started smoking the cigarettes that Benita left behind. Then Charlie got here and stayed at the house for a couple of hours. He asked me, 'What's the matter with Terry? He should let go of the car. This kind of business can bring real trouble. It was probably cut up a long time ago.'"

"He doesn't know what he's talking about," I said.

"The guy didn't call again, so finally Charlie left for his shop. I just know he had the car. If you had heard him you would have believed it too. He wanted to deal with you and no police. Otherwise you'd never see the car again!"

"Okay, calm down, it's all over."

"But, what if he calls tomorrow?"

"I'll be home tomorrow."

I got Alice to tell the story over and over, searching for a clue to show me that this guy had the car. She stopped scrubbing a pot at the sink. "This is the last time I'm telling you."

The only thing that sounded encouraging was the fact that the guy knew that the Vette was from Sixty-fourth Street in Brooklyn. That information was not on the reward poster or in the newspapers. He could've gotten it from the license plate but then he would have to have access to the police computer and I knew how difficult that could be. There were several bills and letters with our address on them in the car when it was stolen. I figured that was how this guy knew where we lived.

"How did he sound?"

"Spanish."

"That's all? You can't tell me anything else?"

"That's it! I don't want to talk about it any more."

ELECTRIC THIEF

I WAS RELUCTANT TO LEAVE the house the next day thinking that Sam Ashkin or the Spanish guy might call again but they didn't. In fact, for the next several days, I heard nothing about the car from anyone. I busied myself gathering more firewood. I had bought a used wood-burning stove and set it up in the kitchen. You could burn coal or wood on the one that was originally there, the one my grandfather had used. There are three entrances to our kitchen, so I expected the heat generated by the stove to radiate through the house. I also bought a secondhand chain saw and found where they dump all the tree trimmings from Prospect Park. It took about an hour to cut and stack a carload. I figured with each trip I was bringing home about fifty dollars worth of wood or the equivalent of a week's worth of fuel oil. Mrs. Filo, our neighbor, was usually at her window watching me unload the car. She had already complained to Alice that the ashes from our stove fouled up her clothesline.

Mrs. Lantini, a widow, had an old frame house on Seventeenth Avenue that was divided up into several apartments. I had been doing some small electrical jobs to make money and she had been trying to get me to come over for weeks but I just kept putting it off. When I finally rang her doorbell she was so happy to see me that she put her old face with its hairy moles to mine and gave me a revolting wet kiss on the cheek.

"What's the problem, Mrs. Lantini?"

"Come in, Terry. I'll tell you all about it. You want some soda—a beer?"

"No thanks. What's wrong that you want me to fix?"

"What's wrong? I'll tell you what's wrong! That piece of furniture on the second floor isn't paying for her electricity! That's what's wrong! She says she's been paying for the lights in the hall when she's not supposed to, but that's not true. I told her I pay for the lights in the hall. She hasn't paid her electric for the last three months. She's supposed to pay it to me, you know, then I pay for the whole house."

"What do you want me to do?"

"I took out the fuse but she still has electricity in her apartment. There shouldn't be any but there is."

"Sounds like a job for Con Edison."

"They say only if she had a meter could they turn it off."

"Right."

"I want you to find how the electricity is going to her apartment—and cut it off!"

"I don't want to get involved in this."

"Terry, I'm an old woman—an old customer! She didn't pay her bill!"

"Okay."

"You hear that radio playing loud? That's her. She's just doing it to show me."

We went down the cellar and Mrs. Lantini waddled over to the fuse box that she had turned off. "This is the one," she said.

I spent a half hour tracing out lines with the old lady breathing down my neck and complaining about the tenant.

"Please, I can't concentrate."

"Excuse me."

I found a lead going into the ceiling that looked like the culprit.

"Cut it off! Cut it off!" she said.

I disconnected the wires in the junction box and put the cover back on. We went upstairs. The radio was playing even louder than before.

"Maybe it's a portable."

"No, I've seen the radio. It's not a portable."

I stepped outside and looked up to the second floor where the noise was coming from. There was a florescent light on in the kitchen. Someone was looking out from behind the curtain. I went back inside to Mrs. Lantini. "Yeah, she still has electricity."

"I know. What can we do, Terry?"

I went downstairs and began to trace out the spaghetti again. It wasn't easy in an old house where a lot of changes have been made. By the looks of the wiring, she'd had some shoemakers working for her for sure. I couldn't understand it. There were no other live lines going up to the second-floor front. Then I found a wire plugged into Mrs. Lantini's washing machine outlet and running out the cellar window and up the side of the house. "This has to be it," I told the old lady. Her eyes twinkled. I pulled the plug, climbed the stairs and went out into the street. The radio was off but the light was still on. I went downstairs again and shook my head to Mrs. Lantini.

"What can we do, Terry?"

"If I cut any more lines we'll be shutting someone else off."

"We can't do that."

"I know."

"Are you a landlord, Terry?"

"No."

"Don't ever be landlord."

"Have her thrown out."

"Easy to say."

"I have to go. I can't do anything more here."

"Just try one more time."

"No."

"Please. For an old woman, an old customer!"

"All right, but you're wasting money." I went down the cellar again and started searching. It was now a challenge. I wanted to prove that they couldn't outsmart the electrician but after looking for a long time I didn't find any other possibilities. Maybe the tenant had some hotshot come in when Mrs. Lantini was out shopping and the guy sneaked something through. I should have found it. Later, I climbed the stairs and entered the kitchen where the old lady was having tea with anisette toast. "She could be getting juice from another apartment."

"Nah, they wouldn't give it to her," Mrs. Lantini said while dunking the toast into the steaming cup. "They don't get along—want some tea?"

"No thanks. I can't figure it out then."

"With all your experience?"

"That's right. I could spend hours here and still not find anything in this old house."

"You don't like my house?"

"I'll just charge you the minimum—an hour's time."

"How can you charge me when you haven't even turned her lights off?"

"Hey, I can't work for nothing."

"I have to pay you and pay her electric bill too?"

"Forget about it, Mrs. Lantini. I knew I shouldn't have come here. This place is always a headache."

"Oh, don't talk like that. What happened to you? You were always such a nice guy!"

I left the kitchen with my tool pouch, walked out into the street, and looked up to the second floor for a last time. The radio was blasting again and the florescent light was on. There was a heavily made-up woman about fifty years old at the window. She stuck her tongue out at me. I made a scissor sign with my fingers and headed for my car.

RANSOM

ONE MORNING in the middle of November I got a call from Sam Ashkin's partner. He related what transpired during the first phone conversation, so I knew he and Ashkin were connected. I blasted him about the phony names his partner had given me but didn't go too far because he was in control. If he hung up, that was it.

"How come you're so sure the VIN you gave us was put on your car?" he asked.

I was careful not to give too much information like the last time. "It was registered only three weeks after mine was stolen."

"That doesn't mean anything," he said

"There's more."

"It could all be coincidence. Most old Corvettes have been stolen somewhere along the line. Where'd *you* get the car?" the guy asked. He had a deep voice with a slow bullshitting way of talking. He sounded about forty-five years old. I heard Ashkin coaxing him in the background.

"It was a clean car," I said. "All the numbers matched."

"It'll cost you more than $1,000 to get it back."

"I'm unemployed! That's the best I can do!"

"Easy. Don't get so worked up over a lousy car."

I wanted to tell this guy he was an asshole but instead I told him how long I had the Vette and some of the rest.

"I'll get back to you," he interrupted.

"When? You got me hanging here!"

"Take it easy. It's only a machine," he said and then hung up.

When I first got the car I used to lay my head on the warm hood and listen to the engine. It talked to me. Said it would take me anywhere.

Ashkin's partner was a crook but he didn't sound like a car thief. They must have bought the car from Rubio or Fernandez or whatever the right name was, realized it was hot, and were now trying to minimize their losses. They probably bought it cheap. The price alone should have tipped them off. I wondered where and how an exchange might take place.

I called Pete Rousseau at the auto crime unit.

"A ransom?" he said laughing.

"They want more than my $1,000 reward."

"I never heard of anything like that. You sure you're not making this up? I know you're a writer."

"I'm not."

"They call back again, agree to pay them anything they want. We'll get your car back for you and it won't cost you a dime. Just find out where they want to meet and we'll be there. But, don't go alone."

Maybe Rousseau was just saying this because he didn't think it would come to pass. He could have been just playing along. For days I waited around for Ashkin's partner to get back to me.

I find myself driving down to Bushwick. I left the house with an entirely different destination in mind but now, I've been sidetracked. I turn the corner onto Stagg Street, the brakes squeaking as usual, and immediately spot a red car down at the end of the block. As I grow nearer, the car looks more and more like my Corvette. When I'm close, for sure it's the car. Just the way it sits tells me it's mine. I start shaking and pull the station wagon in front of the Vette, leaving the rear end sticking out in the driving lane. The Plymouth's keys won't come out of the steering column when I shut it down. I reach under the seat and pull out the baseball bat. When I open the door, the lookouts on the corner all turn my way. Two that were sitting on milk boxes stand up. I walk over to the Vette without taking my eyes off the lookouts and lean on the front fender facing "A." Since I've been coming down here I've noticed that a police car passes by Stagg Street or Lorimer every ten or fifteen minutes. If I can just keep them from moving the car for that time. One of the lookouts crosses the street and enters a bodega. There's one building between "A" and the store. Not long after that the door to "A" opens and a figure appears. By his spindly legs and mustache, I recognize Rubio. He walks toward me at a fast clip. He's jangling car keys in his right hand. His other hand's in back of him. He must be holding a knife or something. Out of the corner of my eye I see the lookouts moving in. A guy with a bandanna around his head is at the lead. I've seen him before coming out of "A." I figure this is probably Fernandez.

Rubio's got the keys, so he thinks he's going to drive the car away. I've got to disable it so it can't be driven. I should have opened the hood and pulled the wires out of the distributor but it's all happening very fast. Rubio's almost on top of me. The others are breathing down my neck. I turn and let the Vette have it in the windshield with the bat, not using full force so that the glass doesn't crumble but instead turns into a milky cloud of cracks. Now he can't see to drive. Rubio lunges for me. The bat catches him across the stomach and makes him fold up, revealing the top of his head, which is so bald I'm shocked. A long sharp screwdriver drops from his hand. Someone jumps from behind and is choking me. I reach back and try to pull him by the head over my shoulder but my hands keep slipping. There's blood or grease or something on the back of his head and neck. I'm sure it's Fernandez. He presses on my jugular as I flip his light body over my shoulder. I go down on the street with him clinging to my neck. The blood or grease is on my hands and face and arms. Black specs float across my eyes like feathers. Rubio gets up slowly and moves to kick me but I sidestep him and get a hold on his neck. He tries to bite my face. Fernandez is hovering over me blocking out the light. The others are moving in . . .

I woke up sweating though the covers were on the floor. Jack was crying in his room. I picked him up and got a bottle out of the refrigerator to warm on the stove. When he settled in, I turned on the television in the living room and caught part of *High Noon* with Gary Cooper until I fell asleep on the couch.

On a tip I checked out a Corvette that was in a body shop called De Dentist on Pennsylvania Avenue. The car turned out to be a basket case and maroon in color, not red. De Dentist was not far from Charlie's store so I headed over there for a visit. I had mixed feelings about going. I liked to see him but I didn't like when he lectured me. I never told him how to run his life.

When I entered there were several people waiting at the counter. Charlie's partner and a new guy were working in the back. One customer was getting keys made, a couple were having alarms installed in their cars, another had an empty window frame he wanted glazed.

"Terry!" Charlie says when he finally notices me. "What are you doing here?"

"Had to look at a job."

Charlie took a freshly made key out of a duplicating machine and knocked off the burrs with a file. "There you go," he said to the man waiting, and then to me, "How's Alice and the kids?"

"Fine."

"I can't afford to have kids," Charlie said while measuring the frame. "I don't know how you do it."

"We get by."

"You know we could use an extra guy here."

"Cut it out, Charlie, I'm no charity case."

"The offer stands. Wanna cut the glass?"

"You trying to suck me in?"

"Give you some practice."

"I'm an electrician, not a glazier."

"Eh, anything for money. Keep you out of trouble."

Charlie laid a large piece of glass on a rug-covered workbench. His tongue stuck out between his teeth. He set his straight edge and ran the cutter down the glass just once. It made a crackling sandy sound. "Went fishing last Sunday."

"How'd you do?"

"Would you believe—I got seasick? I'd 've given them a hundred bucks to take me back."

"You weren't on your own boat?"

"No, it was the *Betty Two* out of Sheepshead. Mine's in dry dock."

"The best thing," I said, "about having your own boat is that you can quit whenever you want to. It's like being your own boss."

"Bosses can't quit whenever they want to."

"I guess not."

"They got responsibilities. Stick around and have lunch," Charlie said. His impending lecture about me still chasing after the Corvette smelled like bad fish.

"I know your lunches," I said, heading for the door.

"Hello to Alice," Charlie called.

One spring morning I deliberately made myself late for school so that Dad would have to drive me in his taxi. I knew the teacher would be angry and that I would get detention for being late—but the ride was worth it. I ran down the back steps and over to the garage. In order to get the stick out of the hasp on the door, I had to jump up and grab at it a few times. Bugsy came down the driveway as I was dragging the door open. "C'mon!" I called. "Help me!"

He had a tie on and Keds sneakers and his ears were shining. He liked to ride in Dad's taxi too, even if it meant being late for school.

My father came out of the house and walked up to us. It was late March and the air smelled of thawed earth and decayed dead leaves from the fall. "Bugsy, old man," he said to my friend who threw his head back revealing his skinny neck and smiling so that his red freckled nose spread across his face.

Dad went into his "It's nice to get up in the morning" song, his one good eye smiling. He had lost the other in a sand lot game of kick-the-wicket when a stick lodged just below his left brow. Years later he had memorized the vision chart in order to pass the chauffeur's test. Bugsy, who was always enthralled with Dad's Barry Fitzgerald brogue when rendering a ditty, buried his face in his hands.

"Let's go," I said pulling on my father's pants pocket. "It's late!" My friend and I jumped in the back and threw down the folding seats while the car was warming up. There was plenty of legroom. Up front, the seat on the passenger side had been removed so that no one could ride there. Only the trip meter occupied that space. Dad flipped the flag-shaped handle, which started the meter ticking, and wheeled the red and yellow '48

DeSoto taxicab out into the street. Each front fender stuck out separately, almost like a sidecar on a motorcycle. "Now, don't touch that crank," my father warned. "Last time it rained I had a flood." He was referring to the handle that operated the Sky View window in the roof. It was a Detroit engineer's brainstorm—people riding in the city cab would be able to see the tops of tall buildings. Dad viewed the innovation as a leaky nuisance, a target for pigeons.

Bugsy took his hand off the crank that would make the glass retract into the roof like a turtle's head into its shell. Some stragglers watched us go by in the taxi. We stuck our tongues out at them. A bar of sunlight shot between two apartment buildings and through the window in the roof. We stopped on the corner by the school where the crossing guard stood. My father turned the flag on the meter, which made our ride official, and sat waiting behind the wheel.

"You forgot something," I said.

"Oh." Dad reached for his leather change sack and pulled out one shiny dime, my allowance.

"I thought we were supposed to pay you," my friend said looking bug-eyed at the pouch. "Doesn't that thing ever run out of dimes?"

"Of course it never runs out of dimes. Right, Dad?"

"Maybe, if people stop tipping . . ."

We got out of the taxi with our heads cocked and strutted across the street like millionaires. The crossing guard with her white belt, peacoat, and cap—and a mouth full of chewing gum yelled, "Wow! A taxi to school!" It made me feel like a celebrity.

"Now, don't ya be takin' any wooden nickels!" my father called to Bugsy's delight. Then he ground the transmission into first gear. The DeSoto, with a bow of letters spelling out Sky View on the door, pulled away and headed for Manhattan where it would ferry people around town until about eight in the evening when Dad would head home with tomorrow's dime safely secured in the leather change sack.

When I got home my wife was kneeling at the woodstove. There were ashes all around the cleanout door and tracks where she walked out to the yard to dump the overfull pan into a barrel.

"We were freezing," she said. "The intakes were so clogged I couldn't get a fire going."

"Sorry."

"Benita called. She said she had a job for you where you can make good money."

"Yeah, I know Benita's jobs."

"I told her you'd call!"

"All right." I walked over to the phone and dialed. After three rings I got a singing, "Hello!"

"What kind of job you got for me this time?"

"Oh, it's you."

"You say it like I'm some kind of disease."

"Quit the gab, Berkson."

"You're the one who called."

"My friend's opening a dance studio on Eighteenth Street in Manhattan. She needs some electrical work done."

"I can't park in New York without commercial plates."

"You did the last time."

"And I got towed away. Cost me almost a hundred bucks to get my car back."

"You were careless."

"Careless, hell. I lost money on that job."

"Do you want to work or not?"

"If it were in Brooklyn I'd be interested."

"Yeah, Berkson."

"Really."

"Let me talk to my sister."

I passed the phone to Alice who had a smirk on her face, and headed out to the woodpile to carry a load into the house. When I returned to the backdoor with my arms full Alice was just hanging up the phone. She came to the door and opened it for me. "Why didn't you take the job?" she asked.

"Ain't worth the trouble."

"Excuses."

I dropped the wood without bending so that it thundered into the box.

COLD TRACKS

WHEN I FIRST STARTED dealing with Detective Daniels, he told me that he went to Stagg Street to check out "A" but the doors were locked and he couldn't get in to look around. I remembered what Randle McCutchin had said about the police wanting to get the big fish connected to "A," so I figured Daniels was told to lay off. But several times after that, when I passed "A" it was closed and the lookouts weren't there on the corner, so maybe they weren't operating when Daniels went there. Maybe all my poking around after Rubio and Fernandez and watching the place had made it a little hot for them. Maybe they took a vacation. Anyway, for a time there didn't seem much sense in checking out "A."

On Christmas Eve I had to let the fire in the stove burn out and switched over to the expensive oil burner because Lizzie was afraid that Santa would get hot-seated. I had to leave the big door on the stove open, "So he won't get locked out, Daddy." You try to be a little creative about Santa and chimneys and stuff and the whole thing backfires on you.

"Now, you better get to bed or he won't come at all," I told her.

Alice was in the attic wrapping presents. I hoped she wouldn't disturb my Corvette notes. Jack had a cold and was sleeping with the vaporizer gurgling away. My wife came down the stairs and saw me moping around the kitchen.

"What's the matter with you, Terry?"

"I don't know."

"Look, it's Christmas. Let's make the most of it."

"You're right."

"How about making me a drink?" she said.

"Good idea."

"One of your highballs with the orange peel rubbed around the rim of the glass."

"I'll have one too."

A few drinks later we were decorating the tree and Alice was standing on a ladder knocking more balls off than she was putting on. She started laughing.

"I don't think it's funny."

"Terry, you're depressing. Do you know that?"

"You're drunk."

"No, I'm not drunk. I'm just telling you what I think. You're such a dud—so heavy."

"What can I do?"

Alice arched her back and wiggled her butt. I picked her off the ladder and carried her to the couch. "This gift I won't have to wrap," she said.

Later, when everyone was sleeping I got the insert soles out of my hunting boots and sprinkled ashes over them to make tracks leading from the stove to the tree.

Late one afternoon, a few weeks later, I was on Stagg Street, a short block from "A". The lookouts seemed especially alert so I watched closely while standing near some street construction. There were two trucks outside the garage. I felt something was going to happen. It was about the time the police change shifts—a good time to move stolen cars and parts. The trucks in front of "A" weren't big enough to carry a whole car, but a nose would easily fit inside either of them. McCutchin told me that "A" had the reputation for being a chop shop. I thought of the chainsaw noise I had heard inside. The men on the corner were looking in all directions. None of them were sitting on their usual milk boxes. Besides the two larger trucks, there was a beige van with curtains on the windows. I knew it was connected to "A" because I'd seen it parked there several times. I was positive something was going to happen. Someone from "A" kept coming out through the man-sized door and looking around. Maybe they were going to move the Vette out in pieces. I was afraid I might see part of my car carried out. There was a pay phone on the corner nearby. I got through to Rousseau easily for a change.

"Have you seen anything—any parts?" he asked.

"No. But I'm positive they're going to make some kind of move."

"I can't send a man down there on a hunch."

"It's no hunch."

"Kid, you're letting your imagination run away with you."

Just then something made me turn around. The beige van from "A" backed up to within twenty feet of me. It sat there idling. Someone lifted a curtain on the truck's side window.

"They sneaked up on me with a van," I said. "I saw a curtain move."

"Hang up and get out of there," Rousseau said. He was trying to humor me. He just wanted to get me off the phone.

"Hey, don't you believe me?"

"I believe you, now get out of there."

I put the receiver down and turned toward the van. It moved away slowly. I knew "A" was going to move something out but the police just didn't give a damn. Nothing was going to be brought out until I left.

When I got back to my car two tires were flat, one with a cut in the sidewall. It looked like sabotage. They knew my car by now. It would only have taken a few seconds to do, but there was so much glass and junk in the street that I couldn't be sure. I used a can of Inflatire on one flat, replaced the other with a bald spare, and limped home.

Often, on my way out, when I got to the back door Bert was waiting there for me, ready to go for a run at Plumb Beach or Prospect Park. But I hadn't taken him with me for a long time. In fact, it had been months since I'd taken Lizzie for a bike ride or Alice out to dinner. All these pressures weighed on me every time I went out, Bert with his hangdog look, Lizzie saying, "Where're you going, Daddy?" and Alice brooding in the kitchen, blowing the hair out of her face, knowing that even without her complaints I was feeling guilty. We didn't talk much—except about phone calls and leads. I told myself I'd make it up to them later.

SMOTHER LOVE

I WAS UP IN THE ATTIC one night going over my car theft notes and updating my journal. Since I had left the magazine this was the only writing I did. Alice was out window-shopping at the mall with her sister. Lizzie's giggles bounced up the stairs to me so that it was hard to concentrate. I reread my latest journal entry: There seem to be two parts to my life these days. The car search part and the family part. For some reason the search part sounds more real. . .

I heard the downstairs backdoor slam and I knew my wife was back home again. She was making her way up the stairs to the kids as I attached the car theft notes to the clipboard.

"Terry! Terry!" she yelled. I dropped the notes on my cot, flew down the stairs two at a time, and ran across the hall to the baby's room. Alice was standing over the crib brushing a towel across Jack's face. There was a cloud of smoke or dust in the air. Alice and Lizzie were crying. I looked down at the baby. He was covered with talcum powder. His face looked like a death mask. It was in his eyes and ears and nose and mouth and he wasn't breathing. He must have sucked more and more powder in every time he attempted to cry as Lizzie kept pouring it on. Alice was trying to clear it out of his mouth so he could take in some air.

"You were supposed to be watching them," Alice said.

Every time Jack tried to breathe he sucked some powder into his lungs. If I gave him mouth to mouth it might force more powder in. Alice turned him on his side and ran a hooked finger through his mouth several times. "Oh, my baby," she kept saying. Lizzie cried louder. Alice picked Jack up and patted him on the back as he hung on her shoulder. He began to gag and tried to cry but he couldn't. He took in a squeaking scoop of air with some powder that was still above his lip. We wrapped him in a blanket and rushed him to the hospital. I drove to Community Hospital on Kings Highway, out of habit I guess because Dad had been there, instead of Maimonides, which is better geared for handling children. Jack's breathing came fast and wheezy.

The young doctor who worked on him seemed clumsy and his hands were shaking. I wanted to snatch Jack up and take him to the other hospital. "Are you making any progress, Doc?"

"I think so," he said.

In what seemed like hours the doctor was able to vacuum all the congealed powder out of the baby's mouth, nose, and eyes. Some color began to return to Jack's face. His crying sounded stronger. We were all in the emergency room. Alice was holding the baby as the doctor worked on him. Lizzie was in my arms crying for her mother, but I couldn't let her go. I was still angry with her, but Alice looked at our daughter longingly. "It's all right," she kept saying to her.

"I think he'll be okay," the doctor said. "You can take him home, but we'll have to watch for complications."

In the car Alice asked, "What were you doing while Lizzie was dumping powder on the baby?"

"I was in the attic—going over my notes."

"You can sleep up there from now on."

"Alice, I had an ear tuned . . ."

"You had your ass tuned."

"That's it. I'm quitting. The hell with the car."

Alice looked at me soberly without saying anything.

Three days later Jack took a turn for the worse and we had to take him back to the hospital where they told us he had chemical pneumonia. They sent us home with medication and a list of instructions. I sat with him at night in the cool vaporized room that the doctor prescribed. A dim light was on. Jack's little breaths were short and raspy; his diaphragm made him pant like Bert on a hot summer day. His sleep was restless as he kept turning from side to side like he was trying to wrestle free of something. I had to constantly fix the covers that he kept throwing off. Alice and I took turns sitting through the night.

How could I undo what I let happen to my son? For a long time I'd been feeling so powerless. Just about the time that we knew for sure Alice was expecting this second baby was when Dad died. If only I had told him the good news right away. Though he was ailing, I'm sure he would have stuck around to see his first grandson. He could have done that because he had endured a hard life of sickness and loss that would have broken a lesser man.

I constantly fluctuated between thinking that the car Rubio was spotted in was definitely mine and what Tamerack and Pete Rousseau said about there being lots of cars like it. The doubtful moments made me follow other leads. As time passed, instead of letting up on the search I went at it harder. I spent most of February and March out every day, cruising neighborhoods, checking dumping grounds, talking to anyone who might know anything about stolen cars. I visited several places almost regularly. They all did work on Corvettes. I went not so much to check them out but to be where I felt closer to my car. I showed whoever was there the reward poster if one wasn't already hanging and, of course, the photographs. Guys liked to talk, so occasionally what seemed like a lead seeped out in conversation. One guy at Corvette Corner on Fourth Avenue sent me all the way out to the southern tip of Staten Island to look at a piece of red fiberglass sticking out of the water. The sky was solid grey. It was high tide so there was just a little piece of what looked like a fender showing, but a local fisherman I talked to told me that the piece had been there since before my Vette was stolen.

One Thursday afternoon, I drove down to Dean Street to report for my last unemployment check. Though a family of four can't live on ninety-five dollars a week, the check was a big help.

Depression set in after I signed for the check and made my way back to the car. I felt hollow, as if I'd graduated from something. To feel better, I got on the Prospect Expressway and headed east for the Jamaica Bay Riding Academy as I had done many times with the Corvette. I looked at my hands positioned on the steering wheel just like my father's used to be. He would drive like this, lost in thought for hours. When I was a kid I'd often wonder what he was thinking about. Maybe it was about my mother who had had a nervous breakdown several years before and was still in the hospital.

He used to take me in his yellow taxi to country auctions where he'd buy things that we would need on the farm he would buy some day. Even then I saw the impracticality of some of his acquisitions. He bought a barrelful of canning jars, huge spools of copper lightning-rod cable, a two-man crosscut saw, rat traps, and more. The only thing he bought that I got some use out of right away was a little oaken box that had a beautiful red velvet-lined interior. It also had a big horseshoe magnet and something that looked like a sawed-off propeller. Two wires with metal, jump-rope-sized handles came out of opposite ends of the box. There was a crank in the front that made the gears and the sawed-off propeller turn. The box produced an electrical shock that could knock you to Canarsie.

My cousin Charlie, who at that time was as big as a blimp, lived upstairs and was always on hand to parrot his parents' derisions about my father throwing away his money on a lot of junk. Sometimes it would make me feel bad and I'd wish I knew what Dad had in mind. He never explained anything he bought. But when we brought home the oak box and I showed Charlie the jolt it could give, he had nothing but praise for the contraption. I developed a routine about the box being a mind-reading machine and on that ruse Charlie and I shocked just about every kid in the neighborhood.

One time this kid Anthony came roller-skating onto our block. Sometimes I'd hear him singing opera in his alley. I didn't think he had a bad voice. We got him to come over and take hold of the handles to have his mind read.

We were set up on Fernazzo's stoop with a lot of kids gathered around. The machine didn't always produce a charge. Anthony was just standing there, skeptical. None of us knew anything about electricity, and we didn't realize that his metal skates would ground him more than any of our previous victims. All at once the juice surged through the wires and into Anthony's arms. Usually the stooge dropped the handles immediately, but now they seemed to be glued to Anthony's hands. My cousin was still cranking away his eyes closed in concentration.

Then, Anthony fell straight back, pulling both the wires and the box off the stoop. He was lying on the sidewalk, out cold, his skate wheels spinning. He didn't seem to be breathing. My cousin bent over him and rolled back one of his eyelids.

Mrs. Fernazzo opened her front door and brought out a glass of water. In a few minutes Anthony was back on his skates again. I checked out the box. The wood was bashed in where it had hit the concrete, but when I opened the lid everything seemed in order.

I wasn't sure what had knocked Anthony out, the fall or the shock, but from that time on, when I'd hear him in the alley, he never seemed to sing his opera on key.

Charlie and I didn't use the box again for a long time.

One day, I went looking for it, but it wasn't in Dad's closet anymore. To my chagrin he told me he had given it away. Years later, I learned that the box was called a Kidder Box, named after its inventor, and that it was supposed to be for the treatment of nervous conditions. Maybe Dad had bought the contraption to use on my mother. Maybe he actually went to the hospital and made her grip the handles as he cranked away. Maybe he got rid of it because it didn't do any good. He never told me and she never got better.

Another place that worked on Corvettes was run by this guy Billy who had the most innocent-looking baby blues you ever saw. I had met him before out in Caldwell, New Jersey, at a swap meet where he was selling hot-looking Vette parts, none of which I recognized. Later, I visited his garage, which was only a few minutes from my house, where I passed my photos around. A guy in a Department of Sanitation uniform who was having some work done looked at a picture and said, "This car was in here a few months ago. It wasn't running but when they finally got it started it took off and ran up on an engine that was sitting on the floor against the wall."

"The car must have had an automatic transmission," I said.

"It did," he said.

Right away I thought of the problematic neutral starter switch I had bypassed that enabled my car to start in any gear. It appeared the car he was talking about behaved the same way. This was quite a coincidence and made me ask several more questions, which prompted Billy Blue Eyes to call the guy into his office. I couldn't hear what they were saying but when the guy came out he changed his story and said the car he was talking about was in the shop more than a year ago, which eliminated the possibility of it being my car.

# of MICE

AT THE RIDING ACADEMY, I parked the wagon out front where I'd always leave the Corvette and slipped through a space in the gate. It was almost dark with not many people around and the air was cooling off fast. There was no grass in the area, just sand and horse shit. I made my way over to a large paddock where several horses were milling around. Nearby, some stable boys were cleaning out stalls and graining the horses. There was lots of fooling around and animated laughter. A girl climbed through the fence surrounding the paddock and walked slowly up to a reddish-brown filly with three white stockings. She grabbed the horse by its halter and led it through the gate and over to an outside stanchion where there was a pail with grooming brushes and combs in it. She tied the horse in and began to run a brush across its back. All this time a steady banter kept up between her and the stable boys and another girl nearby grooming a potbellied pinto. With my beard and camouflage hat I didn't look at all horsey so I didn't act too pushy or too friendly or else these kids would think I was some kind of character.

I wandered over to the stable door where one of the boys had the wheel of the feed cart stuck in a rut. I helped him lift and push it out.

"Thanks," he said.

I nodded. He went into the building and began to serve up scoops of grain to each horse. I entered, reached into the cart, lifted a handful of grain and let it sift through my fingers. There were oats and rye and pellets looking like rabbit food.

"Want some?" the kid says in a friendly way.

"Not really."

"Put a healthy canful in Matchin's stall!" the girl grooming the sorrel filly called to the stable boy.

"I'll dump the whole cart in!" he returned.

I walked over to where the girl was working on the reddish-brown horse. She looked to be about sixteen years old with red hair, milky white skin, and high riding boots. She was holding the horse's folded front leg between her knees and digging out some mud packed in the hollow of the hoof.

"This your horse?" I asked quietly.

"Yes, I just got her."

"She's nice."

"Thank you."

"They take a lot of care."

"Ever have a horse?"

"Almost—but we moved back to the city."

Just then there was a commotion over by the barn. The two stable boys came out holding what looked like mice by the tails. They were little buggers with bodies only two or three inches long. The boys passed nearby with the mice stiff and petrified hanging helplessly.

"Not again!" the redhead said.

"Keep 'em away from the straw!" someone yelled from inside the stable. The boys were excited and laughing. One doused his mouse with what looked like alcohol and I saw that it was alive and squirming. The other boy quickly lit a match and instantly the mouse was a small ball of fire. The boy holding it tossed the burning mouse toward but short of, a manure pile and when it landed I was shocked to see that it was still alive and running in circles. It seemed to run around for a long time. What pain it must have been suffering. The girl watched with casual interest as though this was done all the time. It was almost dark now. I turned to see the second mouse ablaze and stealing across the sand, its gate so smooth it appeared to be a flaming ball rolling. The redhead let out an, "Ooo," like she had seen some pretty display of fireworks.

"You assholes!" I yelled. Everyone looked at me with surprised faces. Even the redhead had to quiet her horse, which was spooked by my outburst. I turned and headed for my car definitely not feeling any better.

In April I heard about this big swap meet held in Carlisle, Pennsylvania, where a lot of Vettes and Vette parts were likely to be sold, so I threw a sleeping bag in the station wagon and headed over the Verrazano Bridge toward the turnpike.

It was a long ride but the weather wasn't bad. The parking area was covered with thick grass and tall maples with young leaves. It was the first day of the weekend meet and a lot of campers had already settled in. I found a level spot and with the clipboard under my arm headed for the gate where a smiling country girl stamped my arm when I paid three bucks.

There was a carnival atmosphere with people hawking parts and souvenir T-shirts, hot dogs, and onion-smothered hamburgers. There were thousands of people, hundreds of cars, and tons of parts.

By late afternoon I'd covered the entire lot, which was about a hundred acres. I'd seen a lot of Vettes and parts but only one '63 roadster. It was even red but its condition was so bad there was no chance of it being my car. The frame, the bumpers, and all the chrome were rusted. The interior looked like it had been pulled out and thrown back in again. The paint, what was left of it, was faded from red to orange. There, sitting on a trailer, the car still looked beautiful, like an old ruin or a weathered tombstone.

I drifted around the Corvette area until it was almost dark and then headed for the station wagon and something to eat in town.

At a pizza parlor, a half dozen French Canadian guys were trying to decide what they wanted on their pizza. I had spotted them at the meet earlier. Words like *anchois, beaucoup de fromage* and *champignons* drifted my way. When they knew what they wanted, their smokey-eyed Paul McCartneyish leader stepped up to the counter and began to order.

"Now, stop foolin' around!" the waitress scolded him as he tried to describe the pizzas he wanted. "You ain't no Frenchman."

The Canadians looked like they were going to starve before the girl took their order. "Cut it out!" she said. She thought the guy was flirting with her. I helped out by translating with my high school French. The girl was satisfied and took the order.

The Frenchmen guided me and my two slices over to their table. They had wine there and the one who looked like McCartney poured more than a generous amount into a plastic cup and pushed it toward me. I hit him with a "Merci."

He returned with a "De rien."

The pizza went down easily with the drink. My food didn't seem to get stuck when I was away from home.

With a lot of repetition and sign language I learned that they belonged to a Corvette restoration club in Charlesbourg, and that they were down to buy parts and maybe a cheap car with rebuilding potential.

Their pizzas arrived and the Canadians received them with as much fanfare as a birthday cake with lighted candles. I tabled the clipboard with the photos on it and told them my story. McCartney filled my cup with wine again. His newspaper impression of New York City was that it was a jungle!

We decided to find a place where we could drink and hear music. They had a camper parked out front with a trailer attached to it. It was like a ball and chain for local driving.

When outside, I offered my car as transportation. They accepted, but not before going to their camper for several more bottles of wine.

We found a club at the edge of town that was thumping so hard from the beat of the music that the roof was going up and down. The place was crowded with people pushing the smoke around on the dance floor. The Frenchmen wanted to join in. There were a lot of ladies there. I acted as the go-between explaining that my friends didn't speak English. I even danced to a couple of numbers myself. We brought the girls back to our table. We were drinking wine and beer and Pernod with water. The girl I danced with sat on my knee and said, "Ooo lala," every couple of minutes. She was cool, brunette, and confident like a country version of a gangster moll.

"You know how to say cut the grass, in French?" she asks me.

"How?"

"Mow dee lawn."

"Is that yours?" I ask.

"My what?"

"Lawnmower."

"I heard it somewhere."

Because it was hard to communicate, the simplest comment was interesting.

McCartney stood up and said he had to take a "piss."

"Hey, Frenchy, watch your mouth," Ooo LaLa said.

McCartney saw that she was angry and looked at me questioningly, "Piss?"

"What's he, a pervert? I thought Frenchmen were supposed to be gentlemen."

The other Frenchmen chimed in, "Piss?" so it sounded like a chorus.

"In French," I said, "piss isn't a bad word."

"Oh," she said. "That's different."

"Like shit."

She laughed and got back on my knee. "Ouch!" she said.

"What's the matter?"

"I snagged my stocking on the table. Want to feel the hole?" She took my hand and guided it high above the knee. Her thigh was as smooth as sour cream. I pulled away. We danced some more.

The place was hot and everyone was sweating. Empty bottles and glasses cluttered the table. I was smoking a fat Gauloises cigarette and was by now quite drunk. After several more fast dances a sour volcano began to erupt in my stomach. I felt sick and needed to get outside.

"What's the matter, big guy?" my dance partner said.

"I have to leave, but I don't want to strand these guys."

"Can't keep the pace, hah?"

"The wine did me in."

"We can take the Frenchies home," Ooo LaLa said.

The cold air out in the parking lot was shocking and my head felt chilled. I became dizzy just as I got to the car and held on the aerial as the pizza, wine, and the rest hit the ground. The windows in my car were fogged. I peered inside and saw movement in the backseat. It was a couple. Her head was against the door and her legs were spread from seat back to seat back. The guy's white ass was thrusting into her. "Oh, ou," she moaned.

The guy grunted as the car rocked gently. I was feeling worse than before. They went on for what seemed a long time until I couldn't wait anymore.

"Hey!" I said opening the door. They scrambled to get untangled. It was one of the Frenchmen and a girl from our table.

"What's going on?" she said.

He had a blank expression on his face.

"Gang bang," I announced. That got her out of the car quickly. I offered no explanation as they were straightening their clothes, just started the engine and wheeled onto the road. At the campsite I crawled into my sleeping bag without inflating the air mattress.

Later in the night, the dream kept waking me. The Corvette is lying there stripped and smoking. Nearby trees are tall and frightening. It has rained but the car is still burning— or steaming. There are tire tracks in the mud. The Indian is standing nearby. Fragments of music float up like cinders from the roar of the fire:

. . . don't be late . . .

. . . when the band starts playin'. . .

. . . 'bout half past eight . . .

. . . in a taxi, honey . . .

A thick oily sour smoke drags across my face and fills my mouth and lungs. Everything is broken and lying on the floor, even the windows. "Daddy, Daddy," I'm calling from behind the door. I'm not tied down but I can't move. There's a green glow from leaves and branches all around me. A tree has fallen and I'm buried but not hurt . . . in a taxi, honey . . . I wake up feeling very much alone.

In the morning I had one of my worst hangovers ever. I just lay there on the hard floor of the station wagon watching the sun burn the dew off the windows.

Later, by force of will I made the rounds to see if any new cars had pulled in. The Frenchies weren't around. Maybe the girls took them home to show them their spare parts. By late afternoon I was on the Pennsylvania Turnpike headed back to Brooklyn. The trip seemed to take forever.

At home Alice gave me a cool greeting like I had gone on vacation or something. "You look sick," she said. "Your eyes are all bloodshot."

"I couldn't sleep."

"You're running yourself down. Why don't you go up to the attic and take a nap."

"Our bed's more comfortable."

"I'll bet it is."

"You know, I'm sorry about the powder."

"You don't act like you're sorry."

"But I am."

ISOLATION

I SEEMED TO BE MORE ISOLATED lately. It was mostly my own fault because I avoided anyone who disapproved of my being out of work and chasing after the Corvette. Alice was no longer sympathetic. Benita and Charlie were open and constant with their digs. I got bad vibrations from neighbors and shopkeepers. Tony the painter didn't wave from his bench across the street like he used to. He had been my welcoming committee sitting on his porch when I'd be coming from the train after a hard day of pulling wires. Even Mrs. Filo seemed to give a smirk from her window.

Success was my only salvation. I had to get my car back to justify all that I'd been doing—or hadn't been doing. Then, I'll show them. I'll show them who was wasting his time. I'll give them all the razz.

It was almost May. The long winter had taken seven cords of wood and two loads of fuel oil. My boss hadn't called again. This was good and bad. It gave me plenty of time to search for the Corvette but it also gave me plenty of time to think about it, not to mention the money strain. Luckily I'd been able to hustle up the side jobs to barely tide us over. Freelancing articles would bring in some money but I couldn't put my mind to that kind of writing. I avoided Charlie when he called because I didn't want to hear any more lectures about quitting the search or winding up in the poorhouse. I worried that when I was ready to go back to work my boss'd be disgusted with my avoiding him and wouldn't hire me.

On Thursday nights, there was a weekly car meet at Nelly Bly down at the foot of Gravesend Bay. Supper was over and I didn't feel like staying home. I puttered around in the cellar until about seven thirty and then went upstairs to get my jacket off the tree in the hall. I passed through the kitchen and patted Alice on the butt as she was doing the dishes at the sink. Before I made it to the door she grabbed hold of my jacket and wouldn't let go. At first it seemed kind of playful. Maybe she was finally forgiving me. The kids were in bed. Maybe she wanted to fool around. But then I began to worry about a sleeve tearing off.

"It's my favorite jacket," I said.

"I don't care."

"You're overreacting to just a little pat."

"Oh, yeah!" she said tugging harder. There was the sound of thread breaking.

"You ripped it!"

"So what?"

She pulled the jacket free, threw it on the floor, and stomped on it. It laid there flat like a cat.

"What's wrong?"

"Nothing," she said.

"What do you mean, nothing?"

Alice looked even angrier.

I tried to take her in my arms but she resisted and instead punched me in the stomach. Then she knocked some stuff off the top of the refrigerator. I grabbed her and held her tight. Then her whole body started shaking and she was crying. Bert started barking outside the door. I told him to shut up.

"What's the matter?" I said, but she couldn't talk. After a while she calmed down and I asked again, "What's the matter?"

"Just hold me and be with me for a little while."

"I'm with you."

"No, you're not. We don't talk. You haven't been with me for a long time. Don't you want to be married anymore?"

"Let me back in our bed and . . ."

"Not for sex. We have to be close first. You avoid me most of the time. I just want to know that your here with me and not someplace else."

"You don't understand," I said.

"You think I don't worry about you wandering around the way you do? Remember, you have responsibilities. We need you, all of you sometimes."

"I'll take better care of you."

"It's you I'm worried about. Even Benita sees something's wrong."

"Me?"

"You're going to get hurt or sick or something. Maybe you should talk to somebody."

"For what?"

"To help you."

"Find my car?"

"No, you clown."

"Don't be silly."

"I'm not being silly."

"I'm sorry," I said kissing her swollen lips and drawing her to me.

"Don't kiss me, Terry. Don't be sorry. Just hold me."

We remained there in the kitchen for a long time. Then I picked up my jacket and the other stuff and put it on a chair. I opened the door to the stove and poked the wood around until it started to radiate a lot more heat. Later, Alice got out some photograph albums and a box of pictures that hadn't been mounted yet.

"I'm so behind on these shots," my wife said. "Look at Lizzie, how much she's grown. I think I'm backlogged enough to fill two albums."

"When did you take all these?" I asked.

"While you were out roaming around."

"I'll buy a couple of albums tomorrow."

A few days later I found myself in Coney Island, at Nathan's, queuing up to buy a famous ninety-five cent hot dog, french fries, and a beer. It started to rain so I walked around to the side where the winter enclosure was still up. It rained harder, harder than I've ever seen it rain. Each drop exploded when it hit the ground. A puddle began to build up at the curb in front of Nathan's. It grew fast. In no time it spread way out into the street and two-thirds of the way across the sidewalk. The damn thing looked like a lake.

The rain let up to a normal rate and people started getting out of their vehicles and heading for the dogs and the frogs' legs and the soft-shell crabs. One guy got to the lake and thought about what he should do. Most people were taking the long way around. He had his shoes on but he began to wade through, the water lapping against the shins of his pants. I couldn't believe my eyes, what this guy was doing for a Nathan's hot dog. The man stepped up to the counter like he did this every day. It was interesting to watch how differently people handled the obstacle. Two guys from inside Nathan's, dressed in white uniforms, brought out a pump and set it up to shoot the water across the street toward the sewer. After awhile the lake started to recede.

It was only a couple of minutes from Nathan's to Theodore's house so I drove over to see if he was home. It was raining so lightly that I had to keep turning the windshield wipers off. Water was rushing down the Indian's street. Twigs and dead leaves floated toward the creek, which was only a couple hundred yards away. I splashed through the mud holes until I was in front of his house. Theodore was out in the yard with boots on, pulling on a tarp that was hanging off of his boat. He waved when he saw me. I got out and picked my way across the yard to get in talking distance.

"Any more rain," the Indian said, "and my boat would have floated away."

"About time to put it in the water."

"No, Terry, I'm gonna sell it."

"How come?"

"Too much money. I damaged the lower unit last year. It cost me two thousand dollars to repair. Things ain't so good to afford expenses like that."

"Still recovering cars?"

"Yeah, but it's slow. I'm getting out of the business. It's not worth it any more."

"I thought it paid good."

"Not good enough to be shot at. Last car I liberated, they were shooting at me. There were three bullet holes in the trunk. The bank complained about the damage when I brought the car in."

"What'll you do instead?"

"Sell cars, real estate, anything—What've you been up to lately?"

"Still laid off."

"Anything new on the car?"

"No."

"A lost cause."

"I hope not."

"Terry, be reasonable—here, give me a hand with this canvas."

I stepped toward him as the mud sucked at my shoes. We

got on opposite sides of the boat and pulled the cover tight. The water ran off the back.

"Now, I can tie it down again," Ted said.

"But look at my shoes."

"Looks like you shined them with a Hershey bar."

JUNKYARD DOGS

I LEFT THE INDIAN and headed for the Coney Island
Police Station to try to get into the computer to see if there
were any changes. I had never gone there. It was more than six
weeks since I last checked the police computer to see if the car
had been sold or transferred. Naturally, I went through the
usual rigmarole with a mustachioed cop at the desk.

"We're not allowed to give out computer information,"
he said.

I explained how I had gotten the VIN and that I needed
to check the computer from time to time. He looked like he
believed me but he still wasn't going to do what I wanted.

"There's no way you're going to get into this computer,"
he said emphatically. "You're wasting your time and mine."

I had met some really tough cops over the last few months,
cops who didn't seem to trust anybody and who thought
everyone was trying to pull a scam. I bumped into one detective at the Bath Beach station who looked like he was going to

explode. Some of these guys chased after lowlifes for so long that they began to look like them. This guy was thick and grubby looking. He had just made a bust and he was all wound up. When I told him about my car he looked like he wanted to bite my head off.

"Just tell me if there's been any recent changes in the registration," I said to this stone wall with a mustache.

Another cop had been listening to my spiel. "'Gaw 'head," he said. "I'll take the responsibility."

"Thanks." I said.

"Hey! Butt-in-sky!" Mustache said to the cop who was willing to help.

"Rules were made to be broken," Butt-in-sky countered.

"Then it's your ass on the line," Mustache said as he got up and walked over to the computer. He punched in the VIN I handed him on a slip of paper. In a few minutes the machine kicked back the information. He looked at it quickly. "There's no change," he said. "The car's still registered to Livingston."

"Livingston?"

"Yeah," he said. "And before that it was Fernandez."

"Are you sure?"

"Yeah," he said not realizing that he had given me new information—that the car was now registered to a third party, with an Anglo name for a change.

"What's Livingston's address?"

"Hey!" he said, and I knew I wasn't getting anything more, so I left after giving Buttinsky a thankful nod.

◆

I called Pete Rousseau but didn't get through to him, so I left a message that the car's registration has been transferred, could he check it out. I did the same with Daniels. I hadn't been in touch with either of them for a couple of months. When neither of them called the next day, I rang up Theodore but his mother said he was out of town. I decided to find out Livingston's address myself.

At a police station on Sixteenth Avenue I told the cop behind the desk that I was in the process of buying a '63 Corvette from a guy by the name of Livingston and that I wanted to make sure that the car was not stolen and was properly registered. I gave him a slip of paper with the name Livingston and the new VIN. He fed the information into the computer while I was thinking about why I never used this approach before. A couple of minutes later all the information came back. I looked over the cop's shoulder as the printout came through. Livingston lived on Whitlock Avenue in the Bronx. The car was registered to him on April 7, more than a month before.

"Everything looks in order," the cop said to me.

I thanked him and went home. Still, there was no call from Rousseau or Daniels. They had told me at NATB that Mr. Tamerack retired back in December or I would have called him. Maybe they told me that just to get rid of me. I dialed and got Rousseau on the phone for a change.

"Didn't they give you my message?"

"No," he said. "We've been switching shifts around. It must've gotten lost in the shuffle."

"That sounds good."

"What?"

"Nothing, there's a new owner for my car, one Norbert Livingston."

"Remember, Terry, it's not definitely your car. It might be another car that might or might not have been stolen."

"It was registered only a month after mine was taken—with owners you can never get to see, and what about Nick the bus driver's description?"

"You're right, kid. It looks suspicious. It should be checked out but don't get your hopes up too high. I've seen it before that we were after the wrong car."

Rousseau put another cop on the phone, a field man by the name of Frank Fish. He sounded like he was annoyed that I was dumped on him.

"I'm buried in work here," he told me. "I can't fart without having to write a report. The first chance I get I'll check this Livingston's car out. Be patient."

I also called Daniels but they told me that he had been transferred.

I waited through Tuesday, Wednesday, and Thursday, and heard nothing. It seemed that the cops at the auto crime unit weren't very interested in recovering just one car. That wouldn't make the newspapers. That wouldn't take the pressure off of them. What they wanted was a syndicate bust, netting fifty or a hundred cars like one I read about back in February, involving the Lorenzo brothers who happened to live only a couple of minutes from my house. They were caught tagging stolen cars with VINs obtained from wrecks in junkyards.

I figured if Pete Rousseau or this new guy Fish was convinced without a doubt that Livingston's car was mine he'd make a move to recover it. He'd be embarrassed not to. The only way I could bring this about was by seeing the car myself. Then, if I was positive it was mine, I'd get on their backs and wouldn't let up until they got off their asses. If I saw the car parked I'd call the regular police and let them handle it. There was one problem with the regular police. If changing the numbers was done well, an untrained cop couldn't tell and he'd think the car wasn't stolen. I was also wondering what kind of changes had been made to the body. Maybe all the unique marks, scratches, and repairs were removed or covered up. I climbed up to the attic and made a list of identifying features. When I got to number thirty I stopped. This was enough; they couldn't have changed all of these. Few people know their cars as well as I know mine. I'd done all the repairs. Heading the list of identifying marks was a quarter-inch crack in the windshield. Located right next to the molding, it would be hard to spot unless you knew it was there. I took the list to the bank and had it notarized. This way Livingston couldn't say I went over the car and then made a list. I didn't expect Livingston, whatever kind of guy he was, to cooperate, because he bought the car from shifty Fernandez who was wanted by the law, but I could have been wrong.

It was a long ride up to the Bronx and I hit Whitlock Avenue on the west side and had to drive almost its entire length to get to the east side where Livingston lived. The day was cloudy and it looked like it was getting ready to rain. I didn't expect to see the Corvette on the street in this kind of weather. When I finally got to Livingston's address I parked the wagon at the other end of the block. My hands were a little shaky as I locked the door. The neighborhood was a mixture of commercial and residential buildings. There was a gas station and then an auto supply store before you got to Livingston's house. The name Livingston was on the sign above the auto supply. I passed by without spotting the Corvette in the driveway. It could have been in the garage. I entered a bar across the street and had a beer near the window so I could watch outside. The slow-bellied bartender pushed his rag down to my end of the bar and tried to loosen me up, but I wasn't interested in talking to anyone, especially a guy right across the street from where Livingston lived. He was bound to know him. After about an hour and two more beers I left.

I went into a hardware store near the corner and approached this fat guy behind the counter. He was wearing an earring and had a tattoo of a chain around his neck. "Do you know of a sports car that's for sale on this block?"

"Hmm," he said as he dropped a handful of threepenny nails on a scale. "The auto store has an old Corvette but I don't think it's for sale."

"Is it red?"

"I think so."

Now, I at least knew that Livingston had the car in his possession. I left the fat guy's place and walked toward the auto supply. I had the clipboard with all the information, all the dead ends, all the names and addresses I'd gathered since I first started searching for my Corvette. From what I could see as I walked past, there was only one customer in Livingston's store. I continued on to the gas station. It was closed but there were some kids biking around the gas pumps.

"You know of a red Corvette for sale around here?" I asked.

They stopped their bikes in front of me and the younger freckle-faced kid who was about ten looked to the other for the answer.

"We don't know of any Corvettes around here," the bigger kid said as they took off. I thought maybe they would know where the car was garaged so I could get a look at it.

I risked blowing my cover and went into Livingston's store, which was crammed with car cosmetics and batteries and brake drums to be ground. The one customer I had seen earlier turned out to be a salesman taking an order.

"What can I do for you?" the guy behind the counter said.

"I'm looking for Norbert Livingston."

The guy's face got red. "What do you want him for?" he asked in a vaguely familiar voice. He was about forty-five with a thick neck, flat nose, and shallow eyes.

"It's about a car," I said as the little freckle-faced kid came out from the back of the store.

"That's him," he said to the man behind the counter as he pointed in my direction.

"My son ain't here," he said a little more excited than before.

"When will he be back?"

"I don't know. What's this about?"

"I'm working in cooperation with the National Auto Theft Bureau. I'd like to check your son's car out. It's just routine."

"What, are you a cop?" the father shouted at me. He was foaming at the mouth, now. I'd shaved my beard and I was wearing my work pants and jacket and my old camouflage hat. "You on the job?" one officer had asked me at the "nine oh" precinct. I'd been mistaken for an undercover cop several times before.

"No, I'm not a cop."

"Where's your partner? The one with the ponytail I see hanging around." I thought of the Indian. Maybe he had tracked the car to Livingston's store.

"I have no partner."

"Come on, you always work in pairs. I know about that son of a bitch in Brooklyn that thinks he's got the new numbers on his stolen car, but he's wrong, because we had the car checked out and there's been no screwing around with the numbers. The prick put out a reward so that my son's been afraid to even register his car. I'd like to meet this guy. I'd spit in his face."

The salesman stopped writing up his order. Livingston went in the back to call his son, I thought, or the police. He came back even angrier than before.

"Where's your identification?" he asked me.

"I have no identification."

He started foaming at the mouth again. "You came in here under false pretenses!"

All the time he was ranting there was something familiar about his voice and his way of talking.

"If the car's like you say it is," I said, "you have nothing to worry about." He had me partly convinced that I was after the wrong Corvette.

Several guys entered the store together. It was obvious he had called them. It was six to one and a couple of them were pretty big. There was a three-foot piece of exhaust pipe leaning against the wall near me. It would stop a couple of them. Norbert Livingston entered the store with his girlfriend. He was tall and wiry with a thin eyebrow for a mustache. They were all circled around me like wolves.

"I'm the guy from Brooklyn," I said.

Livingston didn't looked surprised. He seemed to have known this all along. It would be nice to twist his head around.

I was worried, but I had to carry this thing through. "All I have to do is see the car. I'll know if it's mine."

"There's a lot of '63 Vettes around," young Livingston said. "I saw one in a gas station the other day, original with whitewall tires and spinners just like mine."

The kid sounded sincere. His girlfriend was standing next to him with a sneer on her face.

"Look, I don't want anything that isn't mine. If the numbers check out then you have nothing to worry about. If I could just see it."

"I don't want anything that doesn't belong to me either," Norbert Livingston said. "When we first saw the reward we got in touch with the guy who sold us the car and told him to take it back. But the guy swore that this car wasn't the one in the newspaper. We didn't believe him. He didn't have the money to give back so he gave me another Vette, a dumpy '68, to hold in exchange for the '63."

"Why didn't you call me to check it out?"

"We didn't want any trouble!" the father shouted. "When the numbers came up clean we knew we had a legal car. I even registered the car with the National Corvette Owners Association and they accepted it. They're not going to accept a car without checking out its history!"

"That's bullshit."

Livingston jumped in my face ranting that he was going to sue me. I felt his spit land on my cheek. The circle of junk-yard dogs moved in closer. More spit landed on my face. He was trying to provoke me with six guys behind him.

"Back off," I told him.

He took a swing at me and I blocked it with my left hand as the clipboard fell to the floor. I threw a right that caught him high on his left cheek, making a loud popping noise that I'm not sure was connected to the punch. He stumbled back into the counter. The pack lunged for me as I scrambled for the piece of pipe but it was out of reach so I swept a bunch of cans off a shelf at them and tried to run but they were on me before I could get away. I covered up, taking blows to my back, ribs, and head. A boot dug into my left shin. One shot got through to my ear with such impact that I felt my brain hit the side of my skull as I went down. I heard Norbert's girlfriend scream-ing in the background. Then the front door slammed so hard that the glass shattered. A man yelled, "All right, break it up! Break it up! I SAID BREAK IT UP!" He pulled a couple of men away and the rest backed off while I was lying on the floor with my body throbbing and my ear ringing.

"This is stupid," the guy said to Livingston whose cheek was already red and swelling. I was glad I had at least gotten one good shot in. I moved to pick up the clipboard as blood from my nose dripped on the papers. "Now, calm down and let's not act like animals," the guy continued.

"But Rootie!" Livingston began.

"Wait," the guy said. He was dressed differently than the others, who all looked like laborers. He had on a pair of blue slacks, a blue and white print shirt, and a brown suede jacket. There wasn't a trace of soil or lint on his clothes and his face was clean shaven. He had clear green eyes and a set jaw. I'd seen some cops dressed like this guy.

"You okay?" he asked as he helped me to my feet.

"I just want my car back."

"How do you know it's yours? You've never seen it. All you have to go on is what some bus driver told you."

"How would you know that?"

"Never mind," he said looking sideways at Livingston.

I was thinking there was some kind of a leak or a conspiracy since this guy knew how the car was first spotted.

"You're only guessing this is your car."

"A lot of facts point to it."

The guy was not going to make me feel guilty or doubtful. I argued back and forth with Livingston and his son as the circle of dogs looked on but we weren't getting anywhere. All I knew was that I wasn't backing down. The well-dressed guy looked at his watch.

"Now, I gotta go, and I don't want to have to come back," he said to Livingston. "Settle this thing like human beings."

"Yeah, Rootie," Livingston said, disgusted.

I watched the sharp-dressed guy as he eased out the door. Maybe he didn't want to get any more involved than he already was.

"How come you're after this particular car?" young Norbert wanted to know.

"It was spotted in Brooklyn and registered to two guys with phony addresses."

"That doesn't mean a thing," the father said hiding his cheek with his hand. A mouse was beginning to form under his eye.

"What's the guy's name that you bought the car from?"

"None of your business!" the senior Livingston shouted.

The salesman began to leave. He told Livingston that he'd be back the next day. "Good luck," he muttered to me at the door. I was hoping he'd call the cops when he left. The others were circling around me with impatience. The shortest one lit a cigarette with grease-smudged hands.

"I'll show you the car," young Livingston said. His father looked surprised.

"No you won't," the father yelled. "The car's not here. It's upstate."

"But Pop!"

"Shut your mouth!"

"When can I see it?"

"Maybe in a few days we'll bring it down," the old man said. "Now, get out of my store."

"Then you won't show it to me?"

"The way you came in here you may never see the car!"

Young Norbert looked disappointed. He wanted to settle this thing right away. He's probably been worrying for months. Now, his father has avoided a showdown.

I grabbed the door handle as broken glass crunched beneath my feet. The biggest of the pack had his palm on the lock but when I pulled there was no resistance. They walked outside with me. I was ready for some more rough stuff but the guy that looked like a cop seemed to have put a damper on their plans.

I walked slowly to the station wagon. It was dark out by now and a light rain was falling. My body was getting stiff and I was feeling totally drained. I wondered what my next move should be.

I've gone in, taken a bite, and I'm not going to let go.

The rush-hour traffic back to Brooklyn was horrendous. I sat behind the wheel, my blood still pumping hard from the fight, as the car crept ahead. I thought of being out west on the open road.

Back around 1960, I religiously watched the television show called *Route 66*. A fine formula: two guys traveling across the country, meeting all kinds of people, trying to leave things in better shape than they found them before moving on. Martin Milner was the collegiate type; George Maharis was streetwise and a little crusty. Their Corvette, not the most practical car to go cross-country in, was a symbol of freedom and mobility with little room for emotional-type baggage, or for that matter Samsonite-type either.

These days, such heroes would travel down the road in a Jeep or a four-wheel-drive pickup. That way they'd be able to take on hitchhikers or lost dogs or whatever any particular episode's script threw at them. But not Milner and Maharis. During one show, they found themselves in an Oklahoma oil field. For lack of an alternative, they used their Corvette to power a drilling rig. They removed a rear tire from its rim and then used the mounted rim to drive a belt that was attached to the oil rig. Simple—here was the Corvette, justifying itself, serving mankind as well as an imaginative story line.

Years later, I lived out my own *Route 66* fantasy when I got my '63 roadster. Friends and relatives criticized the car for being so impractical, which pressured me to prove the car could be as useful as a four-door sedan. One time I drove home from the lumberyard with a couple of bags of cement on the front fenders. Another time I put the top down and loaded three ten-foot Lombardy poplars onto the jack storage cover behind the seats. Each burlap ball around the trees' roots weighed more than forty pounds.

This evidence notwithstanding, my cousin Charlie said when I got married, "Well, I guess you'll get rid of the Corvette."

Years passed.

When my elderly but high-spirited Aunt Ruta came down from Richfield Springs for one of her week-long visits, I took her for a ride in the roadster. She reads *Star* magazine and always had her eyes peeled for Burt Reynolds. She had read an article in *Star* telling how Doris Day managed to look so young. "She put Vaseline all over her face before she went to sleep," my aunt explained.

Aunt Ruta tried the Vaseline treatment for several months. The pores of her skin eventually clogged, leaving unsightly, oily blemishes that her old eyes couldn't see. Alice and I told Aunt Ruta what she was doing to her complexion and urged her to discontinue Doris Day's magic formula.

"Maybe I'll switch to Jergen's lotion," she replied.

"Let's give you a facial first," Alice suggested.

Aunt Ruta's pride kicked in, "I don't need—"

"Would you want Burt Reynolds to see you now?" That won her over.

My aunt sat on a stool as my wife began steaming and scrubbing her face. "We need some sort of suction," Alice said, discouraged. She was about to give up when I thought of the T junction on the vacuum advance line feeding the distributor of the Corvette. It would do the job. "Let's go out to the garage," I said with my aunt in tow.

"What for?" she said holding back. "Is this going to hurt?"

"Trust me," I said as I seated her in a chair next to my car. I cleaned a long piece of rubber vacuum hose with alcohol and throttled the Corvette's engine up to a fast idle. At about 800 rpm the manifold produced about twenty-two inches of vacuum that created a suction that could be regulated by opening a bleeder in the T. "Are you crazy?" Alice whispered when she came out to the garage and saw my setup.

"I know what I'm doing," I said pressing the hose into her hand.

Alice, in a huff, grabbed it and reluctantly went to work on Aunt Ruta who seemed to shrink in the chair. The contraption worked like a charm.

I took in the scene: garage doors wide open. My frail aunt leaning far back in the chair as the Corvette's engine cooked. My wife busily vacuuming Aunt Ruta's deeply wrinkled face. A dream come true. Just like *Route 66*. My car had become one of life's essential daily tools. Now, Milner and Maharis weren't the only guys to have used a Corvette in an oil field.

"What do you think Charlie would say about the Corvette now?" I asked my wife.

Aunt Ruta's leg kicked as though she were having a tooth pulled. Then Alice blurted out, "He'd say you can get just as much suction from a station wagon!"

RUBDOWN

WHEN I GOT HOME Alice was on the phone getting another talking to from her sister. Benita had always interfered. That's why we had to elope—she meddled so much with our wedding plans. I don't think Benita has ever forgiven me for cutting her out.

"Tell her to get out of your ear!" I shouted. A loud squawk came from the receiver before my wife put it down.

"What happened to you?" Alice asked when she saw my eye cut and half closed and my ear all red and swollen.

"I think I found my car—but they won't let me see it."

"You fought with them!"

"This guy spit in my face."

"Oh, Terry, you're making me nervous. This has got to stop. They could follow you!"

"No."

"Does it hurt, your eye?"

"No, but my ear's ringing and my ribs are sore."

"It serves you right."

I pulled up my left pants leg. There was a deep gouge in my shin.

"Terry, they could've killed you. Why didn't you let the police handle it?"

"They won't get off their asses."

Lizzie came in from the hall dragging a noisy wooden dog. The racket mixed with the ringing in my ear and made my head ache. "Did you fall, Daddy?" she wanted to know.

"Yes."

"Let me kiss it," she said.

"No, take the dog into the hall."

"But kissing makes it better."

"Go out!" I said.

"Terry!" my wife shouted.

"I'm sorry, Lizzie. You can kiss my ear, that hurts too," I said picking her up.

"Okay, Daddy."

We walked into the living room to see Jack in his playpen. He was lying on his back studying his toes and gurgling. He seemed bigger than I expected. Maybe I haven't looked at him carefully lately. There was spit running down the side of his mouth.

"Mommy says he's cutting another tooth," Lizzie said.

I put my index finger in his palm and he gripped it and moved it around like a shift stick.

"He's still a baby, isn't he, Daddy?"

"Yes."

After the kids were asleep I showered and climbed up to my cot in the attic. There was plenty to put in my journal but I heard Alice coming up the stairs so I stuffed it under the pillow.

"You don't deserve it but I'll give you a rubdown," she said leaning over me. "Turn over, you dummy."

"Ow, not on my ribs!"

Alice worked silently for a long time so that the tension of the fight began to leave my body and I was starting to feel groggy. Then she said, "Who's supposed to relieve my aches and pains?"

"If I could only get to see the car."

"Between you and the kids I'll have an ulcer."

"I could probably figure out which garage it's in."

"We got another cancellation notice on the house insurance."

"I'll bet if I hung around there long enough . . ."

"You better let the police handle it."

"I wish Rousseau'd get off his ass."

Alice smacked me in the ass and she was finished.

"Ow, what'd you do that for?"

"Cause you're not paying attention."

"Why do you listen to Benita?"

"She just likes to talk. Her boyfriend's taking her to Acapulco next month."

"I suppose she's rubbing that in."

"No."

"We'll take a vacation too—when this is all over."

"No, then you'll have to work."

"We'll work one in."

"This is your last rubdown."

"What's that supposed to mean?"

"I'm getting tired—I, I want you to find steady work even if it's not with your old boss, or as an electrician. You could go back to writing for the magazine."

"When I'm so close. How can I turn away now?"

"You wouldn't be turning away. Just let the police handle it."

"And what if I can't. What'll you do?"

"I don't know. It won't be good for us."

Late in the morning of the next day I was headed out to Rockaway. I looked at my hands positioned on the steering wheel at ten and two. Dad had driven like this with both hands. It wasn't cool. It was just an honest hold. "Why don't you drive like Charlie's father?" I had once asked him. "He drives with his right hand on the wheel and his left elbow out the window."

"I'm more comfortable this way," Dad had told me.

The sky was a dense gray and rain thumped against the windshield. Sand and scrub pines skirted the road as the hospital came into view. Dad had made this trip to see my mother for thirty-three years. Now, it was my turn. He had always packed a picnic basket with sandwiches neatly wrapped in crinkly waxed paper. I had been jealous of these outings because I couldn't go along. "There's no place to play out there," Dad had said. "I'll make you a sandwich that you can have later. It's chicken salad."

"Wrap it in waxed paper like the other sandwiches."

Before my father had backed out of the drive I was sitting up in the willow eating the sandwich with my legs dangling.

At the hospital, I signed in at the desk and took the elevator to the fourth floor. She was sitting on her bed when I entered the room and didn't seem to notice my black eye and bruised ear. I bent and kissed her French style on both cheeks the way Dad used to and she laughed. Her lipstick was very thick and a color that must have been popular in the forties. Not to make her feel bad I'd wipe the smudges off my cheeks later. "I want you to look into my eyes at least two times each visit," she said.

"Okay," I agreed. The clock was ticking on the night table. The chair I sat in as usual was positioned just so next to the window. "You're more alert today," I said.

"They reduced my medication—I'm less insane in the summertime."

I took out the articles she had asked for during the last visit: a thirty-three-cent pack of bobby pins, a fifty-nine-cent washcloth, a dollar-twenty-nine bath towel, and three pairs of Trenco panties—"the heavy ones for winter," she had said. The sizes, prices, and brands had to be right or she would not accept them. Dad had stored a supply in a drawer in his bedroom at home. It was a worry that when the drawer was empty I would not be able to find the exact things she wanted.

"I brought something to eat," I said. "Chicken salad sandwiches. Alice made them."

"I'm sorry for stealing you away from your wife and your family." She got up, walked to the sink in the corner of the room and washed her hands and face several times. Then she dried them rubbing extra hard with paper towels. When seated, she held the sandwich in her lap but was having trouble opening the newfangled baggie. "You have to eat along with me," she said. "I'm not allowed to eat alone."

"Who said?" I asked

"The nurse."

"I don't see a nurse."

"She's behind the door."

"I brought some beer," I said. "Do you like beer?"

"Oh yes, very much."

"Where did you meet Dad? He never told me . . ."

"Not allowed to talk while eating. I can tell you some-time—on a beezaganz."

The chicken I had just chewed was suddenly trapped in my throat. I closed my eyes, sat still, and tried to relax. "Beezaganz" was her coded word for a trip home. I pictured the house upside down and everything broken. From then on I chewed silently until my food slowly went down. At the end of the visit I kissed her good-bye on both cheeks and looked into her eyes as she had requested. She handed me a list of things I had to bring next time.

In the parking lot, I cranked up the station wagon and headed back to Brooklyn. The car carried me down the road slowly in the right lane. The yellow and black gate saluted me when I dropped in the fifty cents for the Marine Parkway Bridge toll. Later, I pulled a warm beer out of the six-pack I had sitting on the seat, opened it, and took a long swallow. I'd stop at a gin mill in Sheepshead Bay and have a few more. "Beezaganz" kept reverberating in my ear. I pictured her fighting with Dad in our bedroom as I stood holding a too-sweet glass of chocolate milk that she had passed out to me before closing the door. Now, it had stopped raining. One of Dad's piano songs came to me: "My Blue Heaven."

When I got home from Sheepshead Bay I called my father's old lawyer. He said that Livingston had no legal obligation to show me the car because I had no definite proof the car he had was mine.

Still, I'd never seen the car. With the aid of some magazines I had on Corvettes, I tried to calculate the odds that the Vette I was after was mine. There were about eleven thousand convertibles made in 1963. Of these, about 10 percent had automatic transmissions like mine. That left about eleven hundred cars. There were seven colors offered that year. Red was popular, so let's say five colors. One-fifth of eleven hundred is two hundred twenty red roadsters with powerglide. Of these, I would guess that theft and accidents took half. There were maybe one hundred ten cars left like mine— maybe less. If I had access to the police computer I could have checked out all their dates of registration. But, if they didn't register my car, then it wouldn't show up in the computer. Still, out of one hundred ten cars in the whole country, for one to show up just three weeks after mine was stolen seemed too much of a coincidence.

I put the magazines away, called Detective Rousseau, and told him what had happened in Livingston's store.

"Kid, you shouldn't have gone there alone."

"It was already five days since I called you."

Rousseau covered the phone for a minute and then Fish got on sounding grumpy. "It's a good thing you didn't get to see the car," he said. "Because, then they could claim that you came up with identifying marks after you saw it."

These marks would only be necessary if somehow all the numbers matched or if they were all removed. I didn't bother telling Fish about my notarized list.

"I'm going to call the guy and set up an appointment," he said, "so I can check the car out."

"My lawyer says they don't have to show it to anyone."

"Hey, don't listen to your lawyer. They don't show me the car, I'll block the registration."

"But, that could take a year!"

"I don't think it'll come to that," Fish said. "I'll call you when the meeting's set up. I want you to be near the phone in case I have any questions about identification."

A whole week passed and I didn't hear from Fish. I was completely worthless for all that time. I couldn't think of anything but when the phone was going to ring. I'd never been more anxious about a problem because I never had time to stew over one for so long. I stayed clear of Alice, who was impatient with my hanging around. Not knowing for sure that it was my car kept me from calling Fish. I remembered how stupid I felt when the state trooper in Stony Point showed up for the false alarm. Finally, almost two weeks after I went to Livingston's store I buzzed Fish.

"I told you I'd call you," he said roughly.

"I've been waiting on you."

"Livingston has to bring the car down from upstate."

"He's lying. His son was ready to show it to me when I went there."

"Let's give the guy the benefit of the doubt," Fish said. "I think I'll get to see it early next week."

I waited over the weekend and then Monday and Tuesday squeaked by without hearing anything. It was going on three weeks since I'd learned that Livingston had the car, almost two weeks since I had gone there. They had plenty of time to make changes, to go over it carefully and remove anything that might identify it. I was really getting disgusted and beginning to doubt that the police would ever check out the Livingston car to see if it was mine.

Not to annoy Alice, I went out and called Pete Rousseau from a pay phone. I tried several times before getting through to him.

"Hey, does Livingston know somebody in the police department?"

"Why do you say that?"

"Cause nothing's happening!"

"Take it easy," Rousseau said. "You know I've been on the phone with you for months, checking the VIN in other states, giving you my best advice."

"There was some guy in Livingston's store who knew how the car was first spotted. He looked like a cop. Is that what I'm up against?

"No," Rousseau said. "Definitely not. There's no leaking of information here. Maybe someone you know?"

"Impossible. You think I'm stupid?"

"Anyway, Terry, I want you to come down here. I'd like to see who I've been dealing with all these months."

Maybe he wanted to see if I was some kind of nut, I'd called him so many times—and now I was talking about leaks. Somebody had to tell that guy about the bus driver spotting the car. Rousseau gave me instructions on how to get to the auto crime unit. "It's a hard place to find," he said.

"Don't worry, I'll find it."

We made up to meet the next day at three in the afternoon.

FORSAKEN

WHEN I GOT HOME there was a note from Alice tacked on the back door. Bert was standing at my feet with a what's-going-on expression on his face. I read the note to him:

> Terry,
>
> We're going to stay at Benita's. There's meat loaf in the re-frigerator you can heat up for dinner. The hot dogs are for tomorrow. After that you're on your own.
>
> > Alice
>
> P.S. The property tax payment is past the deadline you marked on the calender.

I unlocked the back door, passed through the kitchen and hall and stopped on the threshold to the living room. Everything looked neat and in order but the house felt like something had swept through it. I walked over to the piano and touched off a chord. It seemed to bounce off the walls with more resonance than ever, making me feel empty.

Back in the kitchen I put some water on the stove to boil, peeled a potato, and got the meatloaf out of the fridge. In twenty minutes I was eating. The food went down easily for a change. I was calm but my chewing sounded like a horse crunching oats in a leather feed bag. When I stopped, my ears were ringing. I was missing the commotion that the kids made. They had a way of keeping me from thinking my own thoughts. Still, I'd rather not think my own thoughts than be without them. My family. Don't they know I love them? Guess, lately it'd been hard to tell. I wondered if she was coming back. Maybe Benita would convince her to stay away for good. I didn't know why I couldn't let the car go, but I couldn't. How could she leave me now?

Later as I was on my way up to the attic Charlie called. I didn't tell him that I was alone. We'd been going flounder fishing every spring for years. I hadn't mentioned the Corvette to him for a while. He probably thought I'd given up by now.

"Why can't you go fishing?" Charlie asked.

"I'm working on a rewiring job."

"Can't you put it off for one day?"

"Half their lights are out."

"Gloria's talking about having a kid."

"What's the rush?"

"We're married four years. You already have two."

"I gotta go to sleep, Charlie."

"Sure about the fishing?"

"Next time."

I began to draw up some diagrams that Rousseau or Fish could use to spot identifying marks on the Vette, the quarter-inch crack in the windshield, a fiberglass repair to the door, an epoxy patch on the gas tank, as well as some of the others that I had notarized. When I was finished I picked up my journal and reread the last entry. Then I started to write down the latest happenings. I was tired so I put my head down to rest for a while . . .

Dad used to play the horses. Belmont Park was his favorite track. For years he hid his racing forms in a closet in the garage because my grandmother would get upset with him gambling with the money he worked so hard to earn. I used to wonder how he'd get a suntan while working on the cab.

"Dad, how'd your right arm get so burned?"

"Driving on the Skyway, the sun gets in the other window," he double-talked me.

Charlie had told me that he overheard his father saying that he would often put fifty dollars down on a horse. Dad must have been a pretty good handicapper because in all those years of betting he never lost the medallion for his taxi. I had heard lots of stories about guys losing everything they had playing the horses. By the time I was fifteen Grandma had already passed on and the racing forms were out of the closet. "Walk to the station and get me a *Mirror*," Dad told me one smoggy summer night when he had difficulty breathing.

"Why not the *Daily News*? I suggested. "It's a fatter paper."

"No, the *Mirror*'s better for the horses."

When I returned with the paper he began his handicapping, which he did at the kitchen table in the company of his friend Paul who was a thick-accented French Canadian occupying a room on the second floor of our house. Paul also played the horses and subsequently lost a lot of money. I knew because he kept a whole shoe box full of losing tickets in his room to show to the IRS in case he had a big winner. It was the time of jockeys Willy Shoemaker and Eddie Arcaro and horses like Nashua and Native Dancer. I got to know quite a bit by just listening to them dope things out. One time, Paul kept talking about this horse he liked, Billy H. I had never heard of the horse and took a look at the form. There was no Billy H there. I asked him to show me where the horse was listed. Right away he pointed to a horse named Bellyache. Dad surely understood which horse Paul meant because he chuckled mischievously when I finally saw the light.

Paul went back to Quebec after an exceptionally bad year of betting on the horses. Not long after that Dad sold his taxi and retired. He seemed to regress into playing the horses secretly in the smoke-filled OTB parlor. It was his one big extravagance. I'd never see him doing his old handicapping at the kitchen table but occasionally a discarded scrap of paper would let me know that he was still a sporting man. Once, not long after I got married, Dad suggested we sell the house in Brooklyn and buy a farm where we'd breed horses—racehorses! My flame for getting a farm had just about expired. "What do we know about breeding horses?" I said. "Picking winners is a lot different than shoveling shit and all the rest that goes with taking care of horses."

"We could get a manager."

"Plus doctors, trainers, farriers. It'd cost a fortune."

"Where's your sense of adventure?" my father said.

"Dad, I'm a married man with my own plans."

I wish I had taken a shot at his dream. Obviously, he liked to be around horses but I think what he needed even more was to be able to breathe some fresh air in the country. Forty years of being stalled in Manhattan traffic and chain-smoking those Luckies had taken their toll. Funny thing, once Dad was gone, his idea to raise horses didn't seem so impractical.

The next day I drove out to the auto crime unit, which was located near Shea Stadium on an island in the midst of several traffic arteries. With some difficulty in finding my way into the immediate area, I finally entered the police parking lot. Dad's clipboard with all the information plus the diagrams from the night before were under my arm.

At the desk I asked for Pete Rousseau's office. The guy gave me instructions for finding it and reminded me to sign, so I added my name to the blotter just like a regular cop. I walked down the hall, made a left, and after passing several doors, entered a crowded office. There were a lot of uniformed cops talking animatedly so that it sounded like a football locker room. I had to shout when I asked for Pete Rousseau. A cop directed me to a room in the back.

Inside, Pete Rousseau dressed in suit and tie was writing at his desk. He was about thirty-five years old with parted brown hair, looking more like a Wall Street businessman than a cop. He was just a bit overweight with a hint of a double chin, a thin mouth, and an energetic nose. He got up to greet me and shook my hand with a firm hold. This made a good impression. You have to give a man a grip, not a dead fish, when shaking hands.

"You got an honest face, kid, you belong in there," Rousseau said, pointing to the room full of uniformed cops. "You're older than I expected."

"I wondered why you always call me kid."

"I call everybody kid."

I showed him the diagrams.

"In case all the numbers were removed or made to match, I drew these sketches. I also have a notarized list."

"You really want this car back," Pete Rousseau said. "What's the rest of that stuff?" he asked pointing to the stack of papers still attached to the clipboard.

"Every lead, every bit of information in tracking down my car. I have Rubio's description. He ought to be brought in to find out where he got it from."

"Now, wait a minute," Rousseau said. "We're still not sure the car you been chasing is yours. It's more than likely stolen because of its history, but it could be another."

"A red roadster with automatic transmission? Quite a co-incidence that it showed up right after mine was stolen."

"Who says automatic?" Rousseau wanted to know.

"Mr. Tamerack from the National Auto Theft Bureau."

"You must've misunderstood," he said. "From the VIN I checked, you can't tell what kind of transmission the car has."

"No?"

I was crushed. I had narrowed it down to one hundred ten cars registered like mine but what he said added hundreds more to my list.

Detective Fish came through the door. He was tall, about six four, and thin with a square, sober, no-nonsense thirty-year-old face. His light brown hair was cut short and his jaw jutted out like someone had just insulted him. He greeted me like I was a crank that he had to be polite to in front of his senior officer.

"Look at these," Rousseau said showing Fish the diagrams and the notarized list.

"What do we need this crap for? The confidential numbers should identify the car."

"Suppose they changed the chassis?"

"Highly unlikely."

"Take a look anyway."

"Sure, Pete, I got loads o' time."

I sat down with Fish and went over the identification I'd noted on paper. I also showed him photographs.

"Ain't a bad load," Fish said.

"I hope it still looks like this."

"How'd you remember all these details?"

"I know my car."

"I used to work on my car," Fish said turning the pages without really looking. "No time any more."

"Yeah," I said.

"Now, you go home," Fish told me when we were finished, "and wait for me to call you."

"You won't run out of steam on this? I did a lot of work to get this far."

"Ey, I told you—I'll take care of it!"

I left after signing out at the desk, got the Plymouth through the surrounding maze of roads and on to the expressway where I headed for the Manhattan Bridge. I reached it just as the N train was crawling off of it into Brooklyn. Trains weren't allowed to cross fast because the tired bridge swayed too much. My car began its ascent over the fractured roadway. Tex Ritter was on my radio singing "Do not forsake me, oh my darlin'!" I looked up at the superstructure with its rust and peeling, faded blue paint. If any bridge in the city is going to fall it's this one, and if there's a time it's going to fall it's right now. I braced myself but nothing happened. In a couple of minutes the car was coasting down onto Canal Street.

Benita's apartment was in Soho on Wooster Street. I took a chance parking in a commercial zone and walked around the corner to her building. There was a guy out front planting an ailanthus tree in a hole he'd broken open next to the curb. His overalls were several sizes too big and he was skinny so his body looked like a stick in a bag. He was in the process of backfilling the dirt. I was tempted to tell him the tree was nothing more than a pesty weed but instead gave him a green thumb up. He looked proud. Maybe he knew it was a weed. I entered and took the old pull cable elevator up to the fourth floor. The last time I was here was when Benita moved in and needed some electrical outlets installed. On her floor the door leading off the elevator was locked so I banged on it a couple of times.

"Who is it?" Benita called a minute later.

"It's Terry."

"Terry who?"

"Oh, come on."

Benita took her sweet time undoing the locks. When the door finally swung open she was standing there in black leotards with her long legs blocking the way. She blew some smoke at me. "What are you doing here, Berkson?"

"I was in the neighborhood."

"Working?"

"Not really."

"I didn't think so."

"Where's my wife?"

"She's inside—doing yoga."

I followed Benita into the living room area. The place was neatly fitted with chrome-and-glass furniture. There were several large blowups of models sporting way-out clothing that Benita must have designed.

"Daddy!" Lizzie called running toward me. I swept her off the floor. Alice looked up from her sitting position on a rug with a sober expression on her face.

"Was in the neighborhood," I said with Lizzie in my arms.

"Oh, really?" Alice said.

"So you're learning yoga?"

"It's relaxing."

"Where's the baby?"

"In the bedroom."

Lizzie slid down my leg like a fireman.

"Could I get a cup of coffee?"

"Instant," Benita sneered.

Alice tried to get up but lost her balance. She was wearing a new outfit with tight ankles and baggy legs—a Benita creation I was sure.

"You're dizzy," I said leaning down to give her a kiss but she turned her head and said, "Benita's leaving town for a few days—a convention in Chicago."

"Yeah."

"Why don't you let Alice go with me?" Benita said. "You can watch the kids for a few days."

"Just like that," I said. "To a party."

"Convention!" Alice corrected me.

"I'll boil some water," Benita said heading for the kitchen.

Out of the corner of my eye I saw Lizzie lift a glass figurine of a nude ballerina off a shelf and hold it precariously by one arm. I saw one like it when I was in the army and traveling in Italy. "Isn't it pretty, Daddy?" There was a small fortune dangling there.

"Oh!" Benita said when she returned from the kitchen and saw what Lizzie was holding. Alice's eyes got wide and her jaw stiffened. Just my luck Lizzie didn't drop it. Instead, she gave it to me. I hefted it in my hands. Then, I bobbled it back and forth. The room was quiet.

"Put it down, Terry," Alice said.

I bounced it a little more.

"Berkson, if you drop that," she warned.

"I want my wife back."

"Don't be silly," Benita said.

I threw the statue up a foot or so. Benita let out an "Ooh!" like she'd been goosed. I threw it up again—even higher. "You're a maniac!" she said. I threw it up again putting a little spin on it this time. It landed in my hands awkwardly. "Put it down, Berkson!" she shouted.

"Think I can't catch?" I said throwing it up again.

"Let's talk," Alice said.

"What's to talk about?"

"Stop playing detective."

"Playing?"

"You have to go to work—right away."

"I will."

"Don't believe him," Benita butted in.

"Mind your own business," I said.

"Wise up, Berkson. You think you're Mickey Spillane or something?"

I threw the statue up extra high but this time Benita lunged for it, hit my arm, and the figurine fell to the floor, smashing into countless pieces.

"You bastard!" Benita shouted as she clung to my shirt and Jack started crying from behind a partition. I was sorry for pushing things too far. Now Lizzie was crying too. "You made me drop it," I said backing away from Benita.

"Bullshit! Get out!" she shouted with tears in her eyes.

"Not without my wife."

"Settle this another time," Benita said. "I'm leaving for the airport in less than an hour."

"You want a lift?"

"You clumsy . . . I wouldn't trust you for a lift in the elevator."

"I'll get you another ballerina."

"With what?" Benita said while fitting a couple of the larger pieces together. "Leave or I'm calling the police."

"I want to go with Daddy," Lizzie said.

"I didn't even see my son," I protested.

"You better leave now," Benita said.

"Now!" Alice shouted.

I hugged Lizzie and kissed her on the head. Alice and Benita were still yelling so I made for the elevator.

I had the feeling that Fish was going to take a lot more time before he did anything. The uncertainty of not knowing whether I was after the right car was driving me crazy. If I went up to the Bronx and watched Livingston's store and house, sooner or later he or his son would lead me to the Corvette. They were probably keeping it in a nearby garage. If they were working on it to erase the identification they must be making several trips to the car each day. If I could just see where they were keeping it. Then I'd wait until they left and I'd peek in a window or a crack in the door to see if it was my car they were hiding. I'd recognize it no matter what they did to it. And if it was mine I would call Rousseau and Fish to tell them they were definitely after the right car. That would get them off their asses. It would be a relief to know for sure. There can't be anything worse than this not-knowing business.

Alice was home again. After a week of being alone I called and begged her to come back. I told her that I would change, that I'd let the police handle things. I didn't know how long I could stand this waiting. If it went on much longer I'd figure a way to sneak out and head for the Bronx.

I once took a trip up to Richfield Springs with my Aunt Ruta riding shotgun in the Vette. "Nice little car," she said when I picked her up at Grand Central Station to take her home. "But, this seat is like sitting in a hole."

"That's the idea," I said.

We left the city to take the Taconic Parkway to the "Rip Fan Vinkle Buddige" as Aunt Ruta called it. We passed through Middleburgh and Cobleskill and smaller towns like Preston Hollow and Lawyersville. I'd made this trip so often the Corvette knew its way by heart. Aunt Ruta had mapped out the course years before. There were no tolls except for the bridge crossing the Hudson. She couldn't get around that expense. "I'm not stingy," she'd say, her small bright eyes twinkling in a squished-up wrinkled face. "Just trrifty."

Uncle William had died several years before. She had closed up her house for the winter, stayed with her son in California, and was now ready to live in Richfield Springs again. I had been elected to meet her at the train and chauffeur her home. At the time I was supposed to be studying for a dreaded science exam. She was a spry old lady then, a real motormouth for the whole trip. When she wasn't commenting on the countryside or gossiping or prying into my personal life, she was cutting farts or dripping gobs of her chicken salad sandwich on my car's black leather seats. It was hard to concentrate on the road. I thought driving faster might shut her up for a while, so I nudged the accelerator toward the floor.

At eighty miles an hour we were passing everything in sight. The Vette was built to cruise at eighty and wind around the rising and falling parkway curves. Aunt Ruta stopped talking and slipped her hand around the grab bar. She was quiet for a long time but out of the corner of my eye I saw that she was trying to read something on my dash gauges, the speedometer I figured. She didn't want me to notice her concern.

We rushed past scores of cars. I was sure she was looking in disbelief at the tachometer, which read thirty-five. She was a spirited old lady and proud of her nerve. Uncle William's cars never had tachometers. My speedometer, which she couldn't see, was holding at eighty miles per hour. We were eating up cars like a hungry Pacman. I acted very relaxed and took one hand off the wheel.

Aunt Ruta crained her neck toward the instrument on the dashboard. "How fast are we going?" she asked finally.

"Thirty-five," I said.

"Oh," she said. "Your Uncle William used to do fifty!"

the LONG WAIT

I'M KIND OF SUPERSTITIOUS about waiting for a good thing to happen. I believe that if you talk about it, it won't come true. Only Alice knew about these latest developments and she'd keep quiet about them. "We don't tell anyone else," I said, intending not to discuss the new turn of events until the Corvette was home in the garage. I felt if I talked about it, the car I'd been after would switch from mine to some other stolen car as Pete Rousseau suggested.

I passed the time cementing the bricks on the front steps and fixing some holes in the sidewalk. A couple of electrical jobs came in from an ad I put in the *Home Reporter,* where I had placed the reward. I postponed going to look at them. The weather was dry and summery as the middle of May was approaching. I felt that my life was on hold. I wouldn't go through all this again. I'd take an old police sergeant's word that I got at the very beginning. "You wanna listen to me, son," he said. "Forget about it. You'll only wind up with ulcers and never see your car again."

I was thinking this way now but probably, as long as there was a chance, I'd go after my car.

Fish called me the following Tuesday. "Just wanted to keep you posted," he said. "Livingston was going to meet me today but he canceled. Said he had to go to Albany to check on something about the car."

"Another stall."

"The guy sounds like he means it. He doesn't figure to be a crook. He's a businessman."

"Come on. All I want to hear is when you're going to check out my car."

"Not yours yet. The meeting's now set up for Thursday in a gas station next to Livingston's store."

"I've been there."

"Stay by the phone Thursday afternoon," was the last thing Fish said.

I expected another stall.

That evening I watched television. It was the kind of thing to do when you were worthless. It did everything for you. I looked over at Alice who was caught up in sorting out the fresh laundry on the couch. Her long shining chestnut hair dropped to her shoulder, half covering her face. She tilted her head and puffed to get the hair out of her eyes. Her graceful hands worked rapidly, folding then placing a shirt on a pile like in some giant game of solitaire. A kind of sorrow washed over me. I was missing the way things were with us before the car was stolen. Her bathrobe pulled away revealing a long smooth leg that tapered down to a delicately defined ankle. It was like seeing her for the first time. I got up and slowly pulled down the window shades. Now, she was watching me.

"I have to get the laundry done," she said.

"You can do it later."

"No, I can't."

"I'll help you."

"How about ironing?"

"I mean it."

"You seem to like the attic. Why the sudden interest?"

I sat on the couch and put my arm around her.

"Watch it, you're messing up the pile!"

I drew her to me and kissed her on the cheek.

Alice held up one of Lizzie's dresses. "Look, Terry, how big she's getting."

"Yeah," I said while easing her back toward the arm of the couch.

"I'm too angry," Alice said.

"I want to make it up to you."

"You say anything when you're in the mood."

"You kicked me out of our bed."

"A long time ago."

I nibbled on her ear and she jerked away. I covered her mouth with mine and she pushed at my chest, her fingers digging into my collarbone, her body rigid. There was a steady pressure from her arms pushing me away. I hummed deeply into her ear. She laughed and there was less resistance. I hummed again. It was like torture to her and she squirmed to get free but I kissed her again and again. I put my face in her hair and took in her fragrance. Now, we were sprawled amidst her scattered game of solitaire. "I'm going to have to fold the clothes all over again."

"Small price to pay."

"Pay?"

The television lurched and John Hillerman came on selling beer nuts. "Oh, John, you're so generous," some beauty said.

Upstairs, there was a wail from Jack's room. It went right through me, "Oh, shit." I pressed on but my son's cresendo threatened to wake his sister and the neighborhood. Alice slipped out from under me and climbed the stairs to the kid's room. Waiting, I began to get drowsy and closed my eyes for awhile.

Before I knew it, it was morning and I was by myself on the couch entwined in the laundry.

Wednesday emptied out like a can of STP. I woke up very early on Thursday morning and to keep busy, prepared breakfast for the family. I slow-cooked bacon and home fries and prepared eggs to order. Lizzie got more on her than in her. Alice force-fed Jack, the mush went in and squirted out again. He reminded me of a fuzzy blond jellyfish. The morning dragged by.

"This is torture," I said.

Alice looked at the ceiling, unsympathetically.

I went out to rake and sweep the yard. When finished I started to straighten out the garage.

By noon I was back in the house. I began to pace the floor. I walked from the kitchen through the hall, out to the porch and back again. The floorboards squeaked and groaned when I got to different spots. They seemed to complain about their wear and my waste of energy. Alice was looking at me sideways. The telephone rang. It was Benita.

"I'm expecting an important call," I told her.

"What kind of important call?"

"None of your business."

"Oh, really."

"About a job." I lied.

"'Bout time, Berkson," she said.

"Don't call back until after five o'clock."

"Let me talk to Alice for a minute."

"Not now!"

"Screw you!" she said and hung up.

Surely Fish would call by five o'clock. If the meeting was canceled again he would have phoned—I'm hoping. It was warm outside. The thermometer was nearing seventy degrees, but the clock on the wall seemed frozen. If Fish felt how I did he'd get the job done. I couldn't help thinking that the sharply dressed guy in Livingston's store had something to do with the delay. Some doubt slips in. I didn't know what I'd do if it turned out not to be my car.

Mrs. Jacoby rang up. She was an old customer and a good one who paid right away, so I didn't want to lose her.

"There's no lights in my house," she said.

"Did you check the fuses?"

"My son checked them. They're all good, he says."

"Are there men working in the street?"

"Wait a minute," she said. "I'll look out the window."

"I'm not going over there," I told Alice. There was a blank expression on her face.

"The only man on the street is selling ice cream," Mrs. Jacoby said. "Can you get over here and do something? My refrigerator is starting to thaw!"

"Call Con Edison," I said. "It sounds like you have a problem with the main."

"Can't you come and check?"

"Mrs. Jacoby, I can't leave the house."

"I'll call someone else, then, if you won't come."

"I'm sorry," I said hanging up. I ripped a beer out of a six-pack in the fridge and guzzled half the can before putting it down on the table.

"Just lost a customer."

"I can't take this," Alice said. "I'm going to do some laundry. Liz is watching television. Jack's carriage is in the backyard. Look out the window once in a while."

"Okay."

The phone rang again at 1:45. I expected Mrs. Jacoby was calling to tell me she was drowning in melted ice cubes, but it was Fish. Alice came up from the basement looking bored. She stood near me at the sink drying dishes she had washed before. Lizzie came in and started running around the kitchen making airplane noises.

"What's that? I can't hear you."

"It's . . . car," Fish said.

"Can you repeat that? There's a lot of noise."

"You heard me. It's your car!"

Alice shrieked and poked me in the ribs, which were still sore from the fight in the store. I heard Livingston in the background. He was squealing like a pig about the money he'd invested in the car.

"I knew right away," Fish said, "when I found the little crack in the windshield. The repair to the door checked out too, and the hidden numbers on the chassis are yours. The others were changed."

Fish said all of this quietly, not to aggravate Livingston, I figured.

Livingston was still talking in the background. Over the phone he sounded like the salesman who said he was calling from New Jersey, and that his name was Sam Ashkin.

"They want to take their tires and mag wheels off the car," Fish said.

"Let them, as long as they put my stuff back."

I remembered young Livingston saying he saw a car with the same whitewalls and spinners as his, so I knew they'd taken them off to put on different wheels and tires.

"Also the top," Fish said. "They say they bought the hardtop that's on the car."

"Let them have it. I have the original in my garage. It wasn't on the car the day it was stolen."

"You don't have to give them anything."

"That's all right."

Hardtops were worth about two thousand dollars. I was feeling generous now that I had my car back. "Let 'em take it. I only want what's mine."

Livingston was still ranting in the background.

"Don't take your eyes off the car," I told Fish. "They might put sugar in the gas tank or something."

"Don't break my balls," Fish said. He didn't like taking the car away from these poor people. But he didn't know about the phone calls from Sam Ashkin and his partner.

"Bring something to cover the car," Fish said.

"Isn't there a convertible top?"

"They say it didn't have one."

"That's bullshit!"

I was sure Livingston was lying, but how could I prove it? I was so happy that it was my car that I told Fish to just drive the car home without a top.

"Oh, no," Fish said. "It has to go to the pound and remain there for ninety days. I'm taking it there now."

"Why? You just proved the car is mine!"

"There might be a claim against it for an accident or something, also, Livingston could contest the car being taken away from him."

I held the receiver to my side. "This thing is gonna go on for another three months."

Alice looked disgusted by the news.

Fish gave me directions on how to get to the Whitestone Pound. "I'm leaving for there as soon as they finish changing the tires," he said.

"Can't I keep the car in my garage for three months?" I asked.

"Hey, that's the law," Fish said before hanging up.

I stood there with the receiver in my hand. "Shit." Fish seemed impatient with me, like I was getting away with something. I hugged Alice tight but she just seemed to go through the motions. Lizzie embraced our legs.

"Maybe now you'll be of some use around here," Alice said.

I went out to the garage to prepare what I needed for the pound. Three more months of waiting, of leaving the Corvette out in the weather was so unreasonable.

With Alice's help, I put the hardtop on the roof rack of the station wagon.

"I can get a hernia from lifting this thing," she said.

"Come on, you're in shape."

"No thanks to you."

After gathering all the rope I could find around the house, I pulled my old canvas tent out of the cellar. I'd cover the car after I put the roof on. I wondered what kind of shape the Corvette was in, and hoped it was still basically the same with the same engine and all. Alice and Lizzie were standing on the driveway as I left. Jack was snoozing in his carriage in the backyard with Bert standing guard.

I got on the Belt Parkway and headed toward the Van Wyck. I'd been to the Whitestone Pound before checking to see if my car might be there. It was only a few minutes away from the island where Pete Rousseau's unit was located. It was about three o'clock. The sky was clear and blue with no clouds except for a couple of streaks left by jet planes. It had rained during the night and now everything was green and steaming with a fresh, clean look that a good rain gives. It bothered me that Fish didn't share my enthusiasm about the car being mine, that he took all my detective work for granted. He seemed to think that Livingston was a victim, that he didn't know he had bought a stolen car. To me, Livingston was a crook—once or twice removed.

I exited at Twentieth Avenue and crossed under the expressway to head down the service road toward the entrance to the pound. When I got to the gate a stocky black cop stopped me. "My car was just brought in," I told him. "I came down to put this roof on."

"You'll have to go in the office first," the cop said pointing to a mobile building set on big cement blocks.

I pulled through the gate and a glimpse of the Corvette's Riverside Red paint grabbed my eye. I stopped, got out, and walked toward the car. The reflection of the sun off a windshield blurred my sight and I stumbled over a jack handle lying on the ground. The car was parked with its nose tucked under a tractor trailer. I was worried that there would be major changes, that its heart had been replaced or something. When I got close I saw that there was a little body damage, also the spinner wheel covers were missing. Livingston conveniently forgot to put them back on when he took off his wheels. It was almost eight months since I last saw the Corvette. If it could talk I was sure it would have some great stories to tell. I ran my fingers across the top of a front fender.

I used to like washing it because I'd get to trace my hands along the beautiful lines. I looked inside. They'd changed the seats for ratty looking '68s. Also the rugs were torn up. There were a lot of nuts and bolts scattered on the floor and in the luggage compartment. I noted that the back bumpers were new, along with the tailpipes and mufflers. They were feeling safe enough to begin a restoration. The front bumpers were turned up like the car had been towed or jacked up with abuse, and my unique bumperettes were missing. Over all, the body, except for damage around a headlight and left back fender, looked pretty good.

A cop came out of the mobile building and whistled me over. I told him I'd be right there, but before I left I pulled the hood latch and looked at the engine. It was mine all right. They hadn't changed the heart. All my care was still inside. I was hoping they hadn't abused the engine. The cop whistled again. I let the hood down and walked to the office.

"I'm Berkson. It's my car," I told the whistler.

"I don't know who you are," he said. "We can't have people poking around."

We walked inside. "Fish waited for you a little while but he had to leave," the cop said.

"I got here in good time."

"How'd you ever find it?" a flaky faced cop sitting behind a desk in civilian clothes asked. "Fish told us a little about it."

"It's a long story."

They gave me a voucher number, 81Z1648, and the date to pick up the car. It was August 15th, a whole ninety days away.

There were no other old Vettes in the pound. My car stood out like a racehorse in a glue factory. Even now, through the office window I saw a couple of guys checking out the car.

"We had a '64 in here a while back," the dry-skinned cop said. "Somehow that car disappeared."

"We'll leave yours right where it is," the whistler said, "so we can keep an eye on it through the window."

"Where was the '64 parked?" I asked.

They didn't remember.

I knew I'd be back the next day with some case-hardened chain to attach my car to the tractor trailer, which looked like it had been there for years, and to chain the brake and the steering wheel together. This would only slow them down if they really wanted the car—and not for very long.

"You're gonna need a new vehicle identification number since your numbers were changed," the cop behind the desk said.

He gave me a form and described a whole rigmarole I'd have to go through including a special police inspection to get the new VIN. I left the office with the pick-up voucher and the new VIN application stuck to my clipboard. There seemed to be no end to the red tape I was going through to get back a car that Fish had already proved to be mine.

The Vette was waiting for me out by the tractor trailer. There were hundreds of cars parked in this tremendous lot. I wondered how many would get back to their rightful owners.

With some help from the cop at the gate I got the hard-top on.

"You better keep close tabs on your car," he said. "A lot of guys are after cars like this."

"What guys?" I asked.

"Believe me," the good-natured cop said.

I knew that I was not going to be sleeping too well for the next ninety days. When the cop went back to his post at the gate I started the engine with the key that Fish had left in the ignition. It was like listening to a voice that I hadn't heard for a long time. There were no knocks but there was a transmission leak I'd have to take care of. I puttered around inside and outside the car for a long time. It was nice to be with it again. There were many wires hanging from where they must have hooked up speakers and a tape deck, and who knows what else to screw up a classic car.

The identification tag under the glove box looked genuine but on close inspection, I found what Fish must have discovered, that they had cut out the crossbar under the glove box with my tag on it and fit in a different crossbar, probably from an old wreck, with the new numbers. I could see where Fish took a knife or something to scratch off the paint where the welds were made to join the bar to the Corvette's body.

The numbers on the engine block had also been changed. The old ones had been ground down and new ones substituted. Only when I looked very closely could I see the telltale signs of the forgery. The scratches where my numbers had been were perpendicular to the run of the metal around adjacent descriptive numbers. The new tag and the numbers on the block were like tattoos, which, no matter what the plastic surgery costs, would have to be removed.

The canvas fit over most of the car and I tied it down on all sides with rope I found around the house. Then I left the pound and headed for home. As I cruised down the parkway I wondered what exactly happened to the car while it was gone, where it was kept and all. They probably towed it away from the hospital, which explained why the front bumpers were turned up.

When Nick, the school bus driver, spotted the Corvette on Stagg Street, they waited a month and changed the registration from Rubio to Fernandez to get new license plates, but I already had the new VIN from Mr. Tamerack's computer and this was like having someone's fingerprints. The car was sold from Fernandez to Livingston for probably a low, no-questions-asked price. Livingston later saw my newspaper reward and called me to check if the car he bought was mine. I told Sam Ashkin/Livingston about the tear in the seat and sure enough the seats had been changed. Also, I told him about the hand-stitched convertible back window and that too was removed from the car.

After Livingston called me, he was absolutely sure he had my car. He didn't want to lose the money he'd paid for it so he contacted Fernandez and told him to take it back. Fernandez either no longer had Livingston's money or assured him that I would never find the Vette if he waited awhile before regis-tering it. Livingston didn't want the car in his possession while it was so hot, so Fernandez, for security, gave Livingston the

'68 Vette that his son mentioned, to hold while he took back mine. Then, if anybody showed up looking for a '63, he'd have a '68 sitting in his garage.

A week later, Sam Ashkin's partner, whom I think was the sharp-dressed guy in the store who looked like a cop, called to confirm that I was after the right car because the number changes, to amateurs, looked so convincing. They had no intention of returning the Vette to me for any size reward. They just wanted more information to see if I had any idea where my car was and to make sure I was not mistaken about which car I was after. When it seemed fairly certain that I had no leads on the whereabouts of the Corvette and Rubio and Fernandez, they decided to take a gamble and wait a few months before registering it—that by then I would have given up chasing after my car.

I wanted to get this all down in my journal. I wished that Fish didn't act like he took the car away from innocent people. Maybe he knew the guy who broke up the fight in the store. The guy I thought was a cop. Maybe that's why he seemed sympathetic. One thing puzzled me though: why was young Livingston willing to show me the Corvette when I went to their store? Probably, he knew nothing about the Sam Ashkin phone calls. All this thinking almost made me miss my exit and I had to brake hard for the turn, which made the guy behind me blow his horn.

The next day, I went back to the pound with two case-hardened chains and installed them as I had planned. Then I drove home and called Pete Rousseau to thank him for all his help.

"You did all the legwork," he said to me.

"You know Livingston's the one that called me for the ransom."

"Be hard to prove," Rousseau said. "Phone records might show it. We'll see."

"What about Rubio and Fernandez and "A?"

"We'll get around to them," he said. "The auto squad has been building a case."

Rousseau hung up. Now that I'd found the car Alice seemed to have softened. I was dying to relate the whole story to Charlie and Benita and everyone who told me to give up, who told me I was crazy, or was just thinking it. I couldn't wait to see the expression on their faces, especially my sister-in-law. But I have this superstition of not talking about a good thing before it happens and the car wasn't in the garage yet.

The next day I dropped by my old shop to see if there was any work. The boss was a bit cool at first because he knew I had been avoiding him for months, but he was about to start a renovation and said that he would take me on for the following week. "You know you lost your seniority," he said as cigar smoke came out with the words. "If we get slow again, you'll be the first to go."

"I understand."

"How's that new baby boy? Have you taken him fishing yet?"

"Soon." I said.

"Say, did you ever find that car?"

"My garage is still empty."

"You could've bought another car with the time you wasted."

"Not the same car."

I left the shop feeling a lot lighter but still concerned about catching up on bills. For insurance I was going to advertise in the *Home Reporter* so that I could get some side jobs for additional income and in case I should be laid off again. I also felt I had a marketable story to tell about the Corvette, but I'd need time to get it all down. Luckily I had kept a journal and saved just about every note and scrap of paper that had to do with my search. I figured in a year or so I'd have it all down in a book.

a SETUP

OVER THE NEXT THREE MONTHS I visited the
Corvette at the pound several times. On one of my trips out
there, I noticed a wrecked, red and white '58 Chevy Impala that
was parked a few rows down from my Corvette. It reminded
me of high school and living with my Aunt Ruta and Uncle
William in Richfield Springs while Dad stayed at a sanitarium
for his lungs. There, one new friend drove a '51 Mercury, another a '56 Ford. Every so often these guys would change cars
like hermit crabs change shells to take on a new look.

My friend Jake was the one who owned the '58 Chevy. He
lived on a farm just outside of town and had quit school the
year before. He had sold a cow to buy this secondhand car of
his dreams. Sometimes he'd cruise past the house at night and
signal for me to come out and ride with him.

Uncle William was a tall, thin, gray-haired old man who
seemed to view everything through clouded eyes. Having
owned his '46 Packard for more than a decade, he didn't
change cars like the guys in town. I was sure he had forgotten
what it was like to be sixteen years old. Unlike Dad, he was
very strict and wouldn't allow me out on school nights. It was

depressing to be in that old house with its large, cold rooms and faded wallpaper. There wasn't even a television. So, I'd fake being tired and go up to my room, drop some shoes on the floor and climb out the window.

One night, hefty Walter Burdock was waiting with Jake.

"Let's get some beer," Walter said when I got to the car. He was always thirsty or hungry but never had any money.

"I've got a half a buck," Jake said smiling, his broken nose pulling to one side.

"Me too," I said.

We drove to Sam Morris's grocery and bought some Topper beer at three quarts for a dollar. Old Sam never checked our IDs and always said the same thing: "Topper beer gives you vitamin P."

Then we cruised around the lake, sometimes speeding, sliding around Deadman's Corner, the beer spilling all over the place. There wasn't very much to do at night in this small town, especially in late autumn. When Jake downshifted and hit the gas, the three two-barrel carburetors on that 348 engine would kick in and throw us back against the seats as the tires barked like dogs and the glass-packed mufflers "burrrappped" like machine guns. There was no car around that could beat Jake's '58 Chevy!

We circled the lake in good time and headed back to town, except when we got to the thirty-miles-per-hour sign, Jake was doing seventy, which we knew would alarm Tank Patterson, the town cop. Sure enough, a pair of headlights went on in Tank's favorite hiding place behind the Agway barn at the edge of town. We were all laughing in the car as Jake slowed down to a teasing forty and Tank gained rapidly.

"Hit it," Walter yelled. "Let's get the hell out of here!"

"Take it easy," Jake said.

"What do cops here do to guys from Brooklyn?" I asked.

"You don't want to know," Walter said.

When Tank was almost on our bumper, Jake made a left turn onto James Street and accelerated. The cop faded behind until his car straightened out, then he was gaining on us again. The patrol car had a siren but I think the ex-stone crusher was ashamed of the commotion it made, so he didn't use it.

Tank had a handicap. He had lost his left arm in an accident while working in a stone quarry. So, when he had to turn a corner and downshift at the same time, his hand had to let go of the specially fitted steering knob, making the wheel spin back out of control.

The town had sadistically equipped the one-armed officer with a '57 Ford that had a suicide knob on the steering wheel and a three-speed shift stick on the column. More power and an automatic transmission would have made him a deadly law enforcer. We rode around town at a leisurely pace, taking extra time at the stop signs, Walter Burdock looking back and laughing his balls off as Tank's headlights grew brighter in the rearview mirror and the whine of his overworked six-cylinder grew louder. The cop must have been boiling behind the wheel. There were no cars or people on the streets.

Then we shot to the edge of town and entered the park. Jake shut off his headlights so Tank wouldn't spot us, and drove by the moonlight high up the rocky mountain road where we could see the whole lake and the town.

We spotted a single car winding and darting through the streets below.

"That's gotta be him," Jake said. "He's trying to catch up with us!"

Walter laughed so hard he pissed in his pants, which prompted Jake to kick him out into the cold night.

"Let me in!" Walter pleaded after a few minutes. Jake shook his head, no. "How about if I take off my wet pants? Would you let me in then?"

"Maybe," Jake said as Walter sat down on the ground, took his shoes off and then his pants. When he approached the car which was idling all that time Jake accelerated just enough to be out of Walter's reach. In a short time, Walter was in a full run trying to catch up to the Chevy with a shoe in each hand and his pants somewhere back up on the hill. After almost reaching the car several times he was winded and dropped off.

"Wait till Tank catches him in his underwear," Jake said. "He'll probably make him ride home in his cruiser—until he smells the piss." We both laughed heartily. Then, we headed back down the hill with our lights still off, the stones thumping beneath the Chevy's tires. Back in town, Jake dropped me off at the house, where I shinnied up the leader line and climbed through the window.

I remember when Jake finally traded in that '58 Chevy for a 409 convertible. Though he loved that car, he acted as though he had forgotten all the good times it had given him. The motor had been run so hard that he had to put 90-weight oil in the crankcase to quiet the bearings. It was one of the few times the car salesman got the oily end of the dipstick.

Later, we heard that the dealer fixed it up with a smaller engine and a new drive train and said that it had belonged to a toe dancer. If Jake had babied that beautiful car, today it would be worth something. But, like most people, my friend wasn't sentimental about this old love affair. It was behind him now. Like a hermit crab, he just moved into something new.

On another visit to the pound I learned that after all the red tape, the new VIN I would get was in the form of a cheap sticker that they affix to the doorpost. If I went for the sticker, the Vette would lose its real identity forever, and as a collector car it would be devalued.

I got to talking with the black cop at the gate who helped me put on the hardtop. He let me in on a technicality to get around having to install a new VIN in order to leave the pound.

"If the car's towed out," he said, "it doesn't have to be registered. All you'll need is the pickup voucher they gave you.

"You'd make a lousy bureaucrat," I told him. "Thanks for the tip."

"Don't say any more than you have to in the office."

"Right."

In about the eighth week of the Corvette's confinement, I showed up at the gate and it wasn't there, neither was the tractor trailer. The black cop wasn't on duty and I couldn't get anything out of the clam that was.

"Son of a bitch. Son of a bitch! The bastards!" I thought back to what the cop in the office said about a '64 disappearing. I looked around. My car was no where in sight. I stormed into the office. "Where the hell's my car?"

"Don't get so excited," Flaky at the desk says. "Which car was yours?"

I was sure he was just jiving me. "You know, the '63 Corvette."

"Oh, yeah, we had to move it to get the tractor trailer out."

"That tractor trailer looked like it was there forever. Even the wheels were sunk deep into the ground."

"Aye, what can I say. It was sold at the auction."

He told me where to find my car. It was now in a spot that they couldn't see from the window. Both chains were cut, the canvas was untied, and the driver's door was unlocked. With what was left of the chain, I hooked the steering wheel to the brake again. While tying down the canvas, a guy driving a huge forklift with a wrecked car in its arms stopped to talk to me.

"A lot of people were looking at your car during the auction," he said.

"It can't go up for sale."

"Even so, keep an eye on it. Let 'em know you're around."

"Thanks."

Leaving it unlocked, unchained, and uncovered looked like a setup. To give the impression that there would be a lot of trouble if my Vette should disappear, I came back with a camera the next day and conspicuously took pictures of the car all locked up and covered. It would be impossible to move the Corvette without the men in the office or at the gate noticing.

Finally, the fourteenth of August crawled around. I made a list the night before of what I'd need to start the car and tow it out of the pound, and carefully loaded all the stuff into the station wagon using up as much time as possible.

I phoned Theodore and he arrived at the house the next morning at eight o'clock. "I'm supposed to be sleeping," he said. "Busy night, liberated eleven cars at fifty bucks each."

"That's good money, Theodore."

"Stealing cars is hard work."

"I thought you should be the one to tow me and the Vette out of the pound," I said. "Without your advice I . . ."

"Me and my big mouth," he said soberly.

I backed the Plymouth out into the street. Forty minutes later we pulled up to the pound gate and a new cop checked my papers. In the office, when they asked if I had acquired the prescribed vehicle identification number, I told them no and that we were towing the car. The cop filling out the release form didn't have any objections. We went outside and started preparing the Vette for the trip. Theodore popped the hood to see the forged numbers on the block. Then he checked the tag under the glove box. "You'll have to straighten these numbers out. If the police stop you . . ."

"I know, I'll get it done."

The Indian nodded.

A tire was low. Theodore filled it from the tank we had brought along. I checked all the fluids and added where needed. Then we jump-started the Vette from the station wagon and the engine came alive. "Success makes everything look different," my friend said over the roar.

We fixed the tow chain to both cars and Theodore in the Plymouth gently pulled me through the gate. We stopped two blocks away from the pound, unhooked the chain, and put one of the wagon's license plates on the roadster.

On the expressway, Theodore drove abreast of me as I sailed along in the Vette, first on the left side, then on the right. The drone of the engine was in my ears. The stiff suspension jostled me when we hit a rough spot in the road. The smell of the sixties' interior filled my head.

OH MEMORIES THAT BLESS AND BURN!

Theodore gave the thumbs-up sign as we went down the road. I tried the radio, which for some reason was full of static. Later, I coasted off the Belt and made a right, heading inland and away from Gravesend Bay. I felt whole again. The car and I had been down this street a thousand times before. I knew I'd been neglectful but now I was going to make it up to Alice and the kids: a new kitchen, no more burning wood, that vacation we talked about—and lots of bike rides with the kids in Prospect Park. We rode under the elevated train and then past Seth Low playground. Just a few more blocks and I'd be there. We passed a stolen car sitting on milk boxes at the curb. Two guys were working to remove something from under the hood. I yelled and shook my fist at them. They looked at me as if to say "mind your own business, buddy." Theodore was watching and ready. I thought of Dad with those long comical strides chasing after the pony and my friend Weenie, and the tall, almost frightening trees on the farm, and the pony. Soon Pellegrino's Bar came into view, its casement windows wide open to let out the smell of stale beer and cigarette smoke from the night before. When I stopped for a red light I was sure I heard a piano playing. The light turned green and I passed Joe The Grocery and then rounded the corner onto Sixty-fourth Street. Tony the painter was sitting on his porch as usual. As I pulled up I imagined Dad standing on our front stoop looking younger than I remembered, both eyes smiling, and Pie Face Freddie from the gas station, and my friend Bugsy in his Keds, and Aunt Ruta holding a bottle of Jergen's lotion. Charlie held the mind reading machine, and Dad's horse dope friend Paul had the *Daily Mirror* tucked under his arm . . .

Then I saw Alice standing in front of the house waiting for me. She puffed at her hair as she gently rocked Jack in his carriage with Lizzie holding on to the side and Bert standing by. I wheeled into the driveway and stopped under the sweeping branches of the willow tree, then cut the engine. The clock in the dash ticked away softly as cooling metal parts began to ping and groan. My family walked toward me in the rearview mirror. I took a deep breath and threw open the door as they grew near.

EPILOGUE

I ONCE READ that if an Eskimo heard a good story that he wanted someone else to hear, he wouldn't pass it on, but would instead ask the storyteller to accompany him on a trip for as many as a hundred miles to recount the tale to a friend. Eskimos consider an original story a valuable possession. Being of the same mind, I found it repulsive when several newspapers and magazines offered to cover my story in an "as told to" format, which would be written by one of their staff writers. I'd be giving away the salt of my experience. Being a writer, I like to labor under the delusion that the end product of existence is story.

When I sent three thousand words to magazine editor John Sullivan at the *New York Daily News* he said, "I like the way the story builds but you have to cut it down to fifteen hundred words." At that time my article just dealt with the nuts and bolts of auto theft and didn't reveal the obsessive dreams, family fights, and the flashbacks. Sullivan let me make all the cuts and the story was a success when it hit the stands. It was even praised on WOR radio. The people who weren't happy with it were Livingston and his friends. Sullivan said that

Livingston called the *Daily News* and complained about me referring to them as junkyard dogs. He even threatened to sue. "Go right ahead," Sullivan said. "If you want more publicity." That was enough to make Livingston back off.

A few months later I made the acquaintance of a tool salesman named Sal who had a red '64 Corvette convertible. He told me that he had bought some things from a guy in the Bronx who told him that the police had taken his son's '63 Corvette away because they said it was stolen. The guy said that some parts from the car were still in the garage and that just having them around as a reminder was aggravating. Sal bought a set of '63 hubcaps and a convertible top with the frame—two things that were missing from my car when I got it back. "There were also seats from a '67 but I had no interest in them because they weren't my year," Sal said. Several years before, I had removed the original seats from my car and stored them up in the rafters of the garage because they were worn. I replaced them with secondhand '67 seats that would have to do until I had the money to reupholster the '63s. After I got the car back from the pound I eventually ordered new seat covers for the stored originals. Before I met Sal, I had already gone back to the Corvette meet in Carlisle, Pennsylvania, where I paid through the nose for a set of hubcaps and a convertible top with the frame. The latches were missing from the top but by chance Theodore had a pair and he gave them to me. Hindsight showed that letting Livingston take his $1,000 worth of mag wheels off my car as the police looked on was a mistake. I believe that I could have kept them because they were on the Corvette but all I wanted was what was originally mine. I later found that all four of my tires had razor slashes in them. The cuts weren't deep enough to cause a flat but they were a worry and I kept my speed down until I replaced them.

Besides repairing the damage, I had to get the vehicle identification numbers straightened out. When the police recovered the Corvette I thought my problems were over. But some of the numbers on the car had been changed, the ones under the glove box and the ones on the cylinder head. If I registered it with the same old numbers and later was stopped by the police, they could impound the car because these hard numbers didn't match the registration. I didn't want to go the route the police recommended and get the cheap-looking sticker that would be glued to the door post. If I agreed to this procedure and accepted replacement numbers, my Corvette's original identity would be lost forever. Also, I was sure that changing the numbers would devalue the car.

I planned to find an expert to grind down the forged numbers on the cylinder head and put mine back. Also, I would have to have a new VIN tag made up to look just like my original. Then I'd be able to register the car as I had in the past. To my disappointment I learned that it was a federal offense to make up an identification tag for an automobile. Even an outlaw I got to know while hunting for my stolen car shied away from admitting that he knew anyone who could make such a tag. After a lot of asking around, I found one guy in a gas station in Bay Ridge who said he could supply a blank tag for $150. Then I would have to find someone to emboss the correct-looking raised numbers. After that, I would have to install the tag with tack welds, which could burn and destroy it, and there was no guarantee that the final product would be a perfect undetectable forgery. I decided to write to Chevrolet about my dilemma. I told them that after all I did to recover my car the police wanted to change its identity with a cockamamie sticker.

About a month later I got a reply from Rick Severson, the area service manager of Chevrolet's New York zone. He said it was possible to get a new replacement tag if I could supply three things. One, a police report showing that my car had been stolen and recovered. Two, an affidavit made out by a manager of a Chevy dealership stating that he went over the car and found that its identity was correct. And three, a rubbing of the identification numbers taken from the chassis above the rear wheel on the driver's side.

Great! I thought. This sounds easy enough. But, when I approached several managers at Chevy dealerships they weren't familiar with this procedure, or maybe they thought I was trying to pull a scam. So, they turned me down. Finally, I told my story to John Barrett at Kin Chevrolet in Brooklyn and he agreed to check the car out. I brought it in the next day and he had one of his Corvette mechanics go over the car thoroughly. He inspected the engine with its forged ID and checked numbers on the transmission and differential.

The mechanic commented that, except for the forged numbers, the car appeared to be completely original. The last thing he did was pull the rear left wheel and put a wire brush to the top of the chassis to clean away the dirt and rust. The man then took a rubbing with a pencil and paper in the narrow space between the metal and the fiberglass. The thieves hadn't been able to change the identification in this tight spot. The numbers came up clearly mine and John Barrett signed the affidavit for securing a duplicate VIN tag. I saved the rubbing to send to Severson, the zone manager.

Now, all I needed was the police report. When I finally tracked down transferred Detective Pete Rousseau, he couldn't vouch for the specific facts and dates I presented because he said, "It's been a long time since the case was closed." Also, the auto crime unit gave me the runaround when I asked for a statement of theft and recovery. It seemed the police were a bit paranoid when it came to supplying information or vouching for somebody.

Then I thought of the auto pound. Surely, they would have a record of when the car was brought in and when it was discharged. I made a trip out to Queens and spoke to Lieutenant Edward Schretzman. He noted the facts and said he would go over my information. If all checked out he would send me the proof I needed. In a few days a police department letter, attesting to the car having been stolen and recovered with all the dates, arrived in the mail.

I sent the required information to area manager Severson. Six weeks later a tag, hand delivered, arrived at Kin Chevrolet for installation by their Corvette mechanic. The procedure caused a little stir. Other mechanics and customers gathered around. Some admired the car. Others asked how I got it back.

No one had heard of getting a replacement VIN tag for an older car. When I later told Theodore about it he was amazed.

There was one disappointment. Though authentic, the new tag did not resemble the old one. It looked like the kind they now use under the windshield in newer cars and was installed with the use of rivets. But, the numbers were mine—and original. Kin billed me for the mechanic's labor, so I have a receipt for installation of a current-style tag.

In order to do the correct job with the numbers on the engine block, the right cylinder head had to be removed. The car ran great so I had no reason to pull the head. In the meantime I removed the forged numbers. The three other locations that displayed the correct VIN would satisfy anyone. If, at some point I needed engine work, I'd pull the head, have the ID pad ground down, and all the correct numbers stamped in. I had just about erased all the physical damage the thieves had done to the car. All that remained was a bad memory.

Not long after I brought the Vette home, I phoned Nick the bus driver and left a message about the reward but he never got back to me. I even left word with some guys at Nathan's on Eighty-sixth Street where he hung out but he never called. Maybe he meant it when he said that he wasn't interested in a reward, that he felt for me, and that he'd kill anyone who'd try to steal his Corvette. Maybe he didn't want the culprits to know that he was the one who first fingered the car. I must have made a nuisance of myself calling him when I thought the car was still at "A" and on his bus route. If by chance he should now come forward, the reward is still waiting for him.

Last year, I finally found my way back to that farm of old—not the exact farm that my father bought when I was a kid but one not far from it and one that he would have loved. I plan to raise a few heifers on it but for now to legitimize us as being a farm I bought a few chickens whose care gives me great pleasure—and fodder for my stories in the local newspaper. The Corvette is parked in the barn next to a stall that will someday hold a horse. Alice retired from twenty-five years of teaching in Brooklyn schools and is now busy trying to make the new house a home. She's also into gardening. Lizzie recently moved to Tennessee with her boyfriend and just got a job with social services as a case worker for children. Jack has returned to Brooklyn and is attending school and working with the handicapped. There's no trace of damage to his lungs from the talcum powder. Last summer Benita came up to the farm with a new boyfriend. She was directly stung by a bee, screamed bloody murder and went home the next day.

Sometimes I miss the old house in Bensonhurst where my family lived for nearly a hundred years. Memories used to course through those oak and wainscotted rooms like blood through a living thing. But this farm, set high in the hills overlooking a glacial lake with cows grazing in the distant fields, somehow makes me feel closer to my father. I've made his dream my dream. The move hasn't been easy but not giving up the search for my Corvette was a great lesson. Like my dad used to tell me, "You want something, be a bulldog. Go in, take a bite, and don't let go." I'm still holding on.